COMFORT EATING

by the same author

How to Leave Twitter
Hungry

Grace Dent

Comfort Eating

What We Eat When Nobody's Looking

faber

First published by Guardian Faber in 2023
Guardian Faber is an imprint of Faber & Faber Ltd
The Bindery, 51 Hatton Garden
London EC1N 8HN

Guardian is a registered trade mark of
Guardian News & Media Ltd,
Kings Place, 90 York Way, London N1 9GU

Typeset by Faber & Faber Ltd
Printed and bound by CPI Group (UK) Ltd, Croydon, CR0 4YY

The right of Grace Dent to be identified as author of this
work has been asserted in accordance with Section 77 of
the Copyright, Designs and Patents Act 1988

Illustrations © Helen Hugh-Jones, 2023

*Every effort has been made to trace or contact all copyright holders.
The publishers would be pleased to rectify at the earliest opportunity
any omissions or errors brought to their notice*

A CIP record for this book
is available from the British Library

ISBN 978–1–783–35285–2

Printed and bound in the UK on FSC® certified paper in line with our continuing
commitment to ethical business practices, sustainability and the environment.
For further information see faber.co.uk/environmental-policy

2 4 6 8 10 9 7 5 3 1

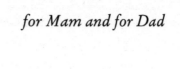

for Mam and for Dad

Contents

Introduction

I am laying out frozen McCain chips on a baking sheet while the oven preheats to 200 degrees – or thereabouts. These chips might go in early, as I'm very hungry, despite having spent a day at the *MasterChef* studios being presented with the finest plates of culinary prowess: a haunch of venison with celeriac three ways with a Malbec jus, and a kumquat soufflé with freshly churned Madagascan vanilla ice cream. It was finickity, fancy food delivered by very stressed chefs, their tension palpable as they entered the room. The eating session was long, with there being four contestants and eight courses, but due to the realities of TV, I only ate very small amounts of very rich things. Now I'm home, and my stomach is rumbling. What I need is some proper dinner, or my 'tea' as I'd have called it when I first began making this recipe.

I need comfort food.

The oven chips are nearly ready now. Their plastic bag is returned to the top drawer of the freezer cabinet, alongside Birds Eye potato waffles, Asda cheese and garlic ciabatta slices, Magnums and a Warburtons Toastie white loaf, in what my other half Charlie and I call 'the Drawer of Deliciousness'. This is the drawer full of things a frazzled individual can rely on when life feels difficult: bready things, potatoey things, buttery things; sweet things to soothe and cheesy things that melt in strings and cling to your chin as you watch *Police Interceptors* on

Channel 5. Sometimes a human being just wants comfort food they can make on autopilot. They want tastes and textures that will fill their stomach and make it tell their brain that everything is going to be all right. 'Just eat your tea,' it says, 'and go to bed. Tomorrow is another day.'

I throw the crispy brown chips in a bowl – they're far too hot to pick up, but I do it anyway, wincing – then hurl Saxa salt at them straight from the canister, followed by some Sarson's malt vinegar. This is no time for the finest pink sea salt fetched from the Himalayas or balsamic from Modena. No. I take a jar of Bisto gravy granules and put two heaped teaspoons into a mug and stir in boiling water. Instant gravy! I cover the chips in the slippery stuff. Then, finally, I finish my *pièce de résistance* with blobs of green mint sauce. Just opening that jar sends me back to Sunday dinners as a child.

I take dinner on a tray to the living room, where I eat it alone, wearing mismatched pyjama top and bottoms, surrounded by the remnants of today's TV glamour: stripped-off false eye-lashes, piles of geisha hair grips, clip-in hair extensions draped over chair arms that look like small feral creatures, high heels, a push-up bra and piles of cotton wool I've used to take off a three-tone eyeshadow.

All these things are fake, just smoke and mirrors for telly. But what is on my plate is sheer reality. This bowl of brown and green is a dollop of nostalgia. It's Mam's Sunday dinners, it's a bell ringing at school in the eighties, and a laugh with friends about last night's *Blackadder*. It has echoes of walking home from the Twisted Wheel nightclub in Carlisle with the lasses in the eighties, too, where a kiosk in the wall near the Citadel would serve pie, chips and peas with ladles of gravy for £1.50.

We'd clutch our polystyrene trays, tipsy, half-naked in spandex, and walk the two miles home in Dolcis kitten heels and body glitter. We felt invincible.

Even though those days are long gone, I'll never stop being fascinated by the things we eat when nobody's watching. They say so much about us. Yes, you could say that we're just mindlessly popping things in a minimart plastic bag, taking them home to be warmed up and eaten. But I've realised it isn't mindless, actually: so often we are recreating childhood or teenage family life, our uni days or that specific flat we shared with our closest friends. Sometimes these foods are plain weird – Hula Hoops dipped in Tiptree jam or custard creams with Primula cheese – but often they're plain things that offer solace: hot buttered toast with the butter spread lavishly under Marmite comes to mind. These things remind you of home in some way, and that is the very essence of comfort eating.

In a world filled with overwhelming choice, there is a pleasure in knowing one's own mind. We are made to feel shameful for eating the exact same lunch every day, or for knowing what we want from the local takeaway before even looking at a menu. We're shamed for being boring, as if the very wise deviate and experiment at every meal. I disagree. Eating the same thing again and again and again and expecting – or in fact *relishing* – the exact same results is the definition of sanity, not insanity.

By now I'm sure you're asking, 'But Grace, what is this book really about?' Well, put simply, it's a bid to understand why certain foods make us comforted and happy. It's about why we lean on cheese, potato, pasta, butter and sugary treats to make us feel safe, and why some tastes, textures, packets and boxes just feel right. It's answering some big questions: why does a blue, yellow and red striped box of Bird's trifle spark joy? Why do the orange parts of a Double Decker wrapper fill me with delight? And why do I never come home after an emotionally hard day and fancy a spinach salad, even if it was whipped up by Gordon Ramsay himself?

I should also say what this book *isn't*. This isn't an excuse to never eat fruit and vegetables because 'Grace Dent said I can live on Rustlers microwavable quarter pounders.' It also isn't a weight-loss or weight-gain plan. It is not a beach body ready cut-out-and-keep chart, nor is it a method to achieve eternal life via bouts of intermittent fasting. At no stage over the following chapters will I reveal secrets to my sensuous beauty via omitting nightshades and legumes or existing solely on 'organ meat'; I also won't discuss any plans to 'enter ketosis' and develop breath like Satan's bum in order to gain a smaller waist. This book will not lead you to be photographed standing sideways in a pair of very loose trousers claiming I changed your life. This book is not a claim that I am any better or worse than you as a human being – in fact, please never see me as a good example, but instead more as a terrible warning. It isn't a lobbying job for fast food companies because I am secretly in the pocket of Big Chicken, and neither is it a lobbying job against fast food as I am also a shill for Big Tofu. I do not think any of the foodstuffs or brands I'll talk about in this book are purely good or bad for you.

I just think that they . . . are.

They exist.

Vividly.

And many of them have been in my life from the very start. As familiar as friends, and as loyal as family. I just know that at

Ramadan, when I see a giant stack of Ferrero Rocher in Leyton Mills Asda, I feel *something*. I feel excited. I don't even observe Ramadan, and I don't particularly love Ferrero Rocher, and I know beyond doubt that refined carbs are not my friend . . . but at the same time there is comfort and jubilation in those fancy gold and brown wrappers. There is happiness, safety, the memory of my parents passing a box around, and the feeling of a treat.

And I just need to talk about it. Especially now, of all times.

On 1 February 2021, my mother, queen of the comfort eaters, finally died, not long after finishing a round of toast and marmalade. I say 'finally' as it had been on the cards for a long time, but as a stubborn Cumberland woman she had more comebacks than Lazarus. The woman was eighty-five and as sharp as a tack until about two days before the end, when she saw my Aunty Beet in the doorway of her bedroom as we sat together on a late Sunday afternoon. Beet had been dead at least thirty-five years.

Up until then, though, it felt like Mam would go on for ever. She had far too much to do: scones to eat, yellow reduced-price stickers to hunt down at Morrisons and piles of Celebration chocolates to feed to her grandchildren. But in November 2020, with tumours in almost every meaningful part of her body, I moved into the back room of her small retirement flat for what neither of us could quite admit was the final push. Eventually we had to name it. She looked at me while we lay in her bed together and said, 'I don't want to leave you all,' and I nodded and said, 'We'll be all right,' as if I was giving her the go-ahead to move on to where she needed to go, saying that I was ready to take it all on, that I'd be the captain. What I really wanted to say as I stood in her little kitchen making toast was, 'Mam, don't go. Please don't go, I can't do it. I don't know what I'm doing. I'm not ready.'

Our last weeks were spent together, and we did what we liked to do best: watch daytime telly about home improvement and eat fruit loaf and slices of pie. And lots and lots of white toast: buttered white Toastie loaf toast coated with the cheap marmalade she loved. My mother's ultimate comfort food was the cheapest of the cheap marmalade, the stuff you could find for twenty-two pence, although she always remembered the halcyon days when she could find it for nine pence a jar in Asda. It was that translucent neon orange stuff that would make Mary Berry weep if she tasted it.

My mother detested the chunky bits of rind that came in 'posh stuff', which she vehemently claimed was the sweepings up off the Duerr's factory floor. And the cost?! 'You spend money like water, you do!' she said when I arrived home from London clutching a gift of fancy preserve from Fortnum & Mason made with organic, award-winning Seville fruit. A snip at only eleven pounds! Ridiculous, she thought. I cannot even repeat her thoughts on the fancy Dalemain World Marmalade Festival, which takes place yearly in Cumbria. For her, cheap, sweet marmalade was comfort in its purest form.

My mother was very proud of what I achieved, the writing and the TV stuff, but she never really understood my fine-dining world. Nights out where fifteen-course tasting menus cost as much as seven days on an all-inclusive Mediterranean cruise? Haute cuisine where a grubby brown smear across a plate was meant to be 'culinary art'? Mam tried to feign excitement when we took her anywhere a bit posh, but I still say her favourite outing out was when we once turned up at a fancy Penrith hotel to find a power cut meant that lunch was cancelled. We ended up in McDonald's instead. I have a treasured photograph of her in a white box jacket and a string of pearls eating her dream dinner: two cheeseburgers, fries and a Coke. She was truly in her element.

I inherited none of my talent for fancy words about food from her. But she did teach me how to make the ultimate Wensleydale and apricot jam sandwich; that the best bit of any rice pudding she chucked together in a big Pyrex dish was the crispy brown skin on the top; that nothing delivers love to another human being more rapidly than someone emptying fish fingers and oven chips into a baking tray; and that there is very little in life not made better by a double fried egg sandwich with white pepper on a buttered white roll. Regardless of what circles I moved in and how pricey the dinners that I wrote about were, she never allowed me to forget what real people actually eat.

I lost my Mam in incremental steps over several arduous, wintry Lakeland days, and it struck me on 27 January, as I was walking around the Co-op in Keswick, just by the trifles, that she had almost completely stopped talking altogether. I was making her comfortable with morphine, and I was grateful she was comfortable. Occasionally she would wake and we'd share an individual fruit trifle, those little supermarket ones with the fruit salad at the bottom and the set custard. We made semi-meaningful sounds at each other, and then she'd sleep again.

There, by the chiller cabinet, I realised that in making her free of pain, what I'd done was a trade-off. She was no longer suffering, but I would never talk to her properly again. She would never again say, 'Is that you?' when I opened the front door with rustling supermarket bags. I would never 'owe' her a phone call and ring to hear her being slightly cross that my fancy London Michelin-star lifestyle had made me forget to ask about her cataracts appointment. I would never get picked up from Carlisle station in her Volvo listening to Max Bygraves's 'You Need Hands', with her saying, 'This is a proper song, you can hear every word!' She would never again call me in the dressing room as I came off live telly and tell me, 'Your dress was lovely, very smart!'

I remember looking down at my basket filled with her comfort foods and realised that this, now, was all we had left. Just eating. And then she stopped doing that.

For the last two months of Mam's life, my actual job, the one that pays the bills, had been barely getting done. I did do a voiceover for a yoghurt company in my little room just metres from where she was sleeping, but I look back now and think I must have been quite insane when agreeing to it. Caring for people is madly expensive, though, so there I was, measuring out drops of morphine, then quietly closing the door, dialling in and pretending to be a happy cow. She would have laughed her head off if she'd known. After she died, for the first few weeks I did very little aside from watch my brother planning a funeral (very diligently) while drinking red wine and eating KitKats. Occasionally I would make a bolognaise sauce and my brother would tactfully adjust the seasoning as, in a fug of oddness, I had forgotten to add herbs or black pepper. My bosses said to me, 'Take as long as you want,' but sitting about drinking wasn't really helping.

One project I had on the back burner was a podcast about the things people really ate. My friend and editor of over twenty-three years, Tim Lusher from the *Guardian*, had gently nagged me for aeons to do a podcast about food. Thank heavens. Somewhere along the way, we formed a plan. I wanted to invite celebrities to my home in London and hold a sane conversation about eating – no restaurants, no diets, no personal chef recipes, just proper eating. I didn't have much more down on paper. It would just be a sparkling, funny chat full of lightning wit and off-the-cuff hilarity. Easy. The biggest problem was that I was at a stage of grief where I couldn't be bothered to get dressed beyond Primark leggings with holes and a cosy, over-sized fishing jumper that I'm pretty sure came from the lost and found box on my brother's campsite. My hair had been in a greasy topknot for weeks, and I was prone to crying at bank adverts where people recite shit poetry over old Britpop tunes. I woke up at 3.15 every morning regretting my decision to be so 'on the ball' about getting Mam painkillers. It was the pain-killers that had sped everything up, I decided. Maybe if I had not been so damned interfering then she would still be here. And why did I admit to the nurses that we needed the palliative care team? Why did I let them say that word, and why did I agree? I've heard this called the bargaining stage: it's a whole lot of 'maybe I should have' and 'what ifs' and 'that was my mistake'. Oh, and in my case, flapjack. That Co-op flapjack that they sell in thick slabs at their bakery counters, in paper bags with rustic names like 'Farmyard Slice', which looks like it might be healthy given that it contains oats and raisins but is actually just wanton syrupy chunks of refined carbs hitting the spot each time your hand rifles into the bag. So damn comforting. My grief settled in just like an extra layer of padding around my bum cheeks.

Despite this, I began having tentative chats with a very organised audio producer called Leah Green. We talked about comfort foods and the stuff people eat behind closed doors. We talked about my frustrations during the decades when I was sent to interview celebs on press junkets because you could never prise anything interesting out of them. What is the point? They turn up with their PR teams and a list of facts about their film that they've already said in eighty-seven other interviews. I'd rather stay in and bake a cake. I told Leah that the most interesting bit of any TV or radio interview I've ever done with any celeb is when the sound technician is checking the celeb's microphone by saying the thing they always, always say:

'Before we begin, what did you have for breakfast?'

The sound person is not interested in the answer. It's just a trick to get a person to say something so they can gauge how loudly the celeb will speak during the interview. I, however, am *very* interested in the answer. It always comes with a backstory. For me, this is the best bit. This is when the perfect, usually guarded A-list entity in front of you suddenly says, 'Two Creme Eggs,' or, 'I finished off last night's tarka dal.' Now that's fascinating. Why Creme Eggs? And who ordered the tarka dal? And where was it from, and do they always order a little too much? Can't we make a podcast where we just talk about that type of thing?

Like I said: privately eaten food, the stuff we cobble together when nobody's looking, is a little window into a person's soul.

Maybe if we asked celebrities to bring something to eat that they would never normally admit to then we'd get a lovely piece of audio that felt as much like a warm embrace as spaghetti on toast. And very quickly, things felt very real. I was going to have to buy some Head & Shoulders, put a bra on and maybe even go as far as some mascara.

Our first booking was Russell T. Davies talking about rugby club buffets and slices of Woolworths pork pie with a boiled egg inside it. Next along, only a few days later, was the comedian Nish Kumar, who bowled in with a yellow polystyrene tray of kebab-shop chips, covered in flappy shawarma meat 'from off the elephant's leg', plus a plastic carton of supermarket hummus which he was using as a sauce. Nish, clutching his secret comfort eating dinner, was instantly more childlike than I'd seen him before. On stage he styles himself as a swaggering king of satire, but now he let me in on tales about his family when they lived in Nottingham, the dreamy summers spent with the twelve of them – mum, aunts and cousins included – sharing his grandparents' terraced house, all sleeping on mattresses along floors and landings. 'We were like mafia bosses!' We talked of the giddy joy of the Pizza Hut ice cream factory and our go-to Nando's orders if we were being 'good' or being 'sensible'. I hadn't laughed so much for six months.

Two years later and at least fifty celebs on, I'm having more fun than I could have imagined. My interview with Siobhán McSweeney from *Derry Girls* (Sister Michael) was perhaps the most life-changing story: here was a woman who had lost both her parents in a short space of time and then had a house fire which wiped out most of their belongings. 'You have to realise, your mother doesn't live in the slippers, Grace,' she said as we sat swigging Guinness from the can and eating slabs of Dairy Milk. It gave me much food for thought, as at that point I was dealing with boxes and boxes of Mam's stuff, including dozens of pairs of shoes a size too big for my feet.

The comedian Jo Brand drove to my house in her Mini, coming directly from a funeral, then rustled up the most exquisite fried bread sandwich, buttery and oily and carby. She was also very wise on grief, having recently lost her mother. I shall always treasure the couple of hours she spent at my kitchen table, talking about setting up by herself as a teenager and all her hideous teenage boyfriends. And I shall never, as long as I live, forget opening the door to the actor Russell Tovey looking ludicrously handsome while clutching a box of Lucky Charms cereal, before he told me a story about an acting assignment that was so filthy it had to go through two layers of production management to be greenlit. Neneh Cherry arrived later in the series, delicate and ageless and very graciously allowing me to quiz her on 'Buffalo Stance' and her album *Raw Like Sushi* (which I have listened to repeatedly since I was fourteen); the thrill of her in my lounge sipping peanut butter and tomato soup with lots of black pepper was fabulous.

The podcast has not been without incident, though: I managed to electrocute myself quite seriously approximately ten minutes before Bernardine Evaristo arrived, but was so determined to do the interview that I carried on – and still rather enjoyed her crisp sandwich with tomatoes, perhaps made all the more delicious by the near-death experience. Tempting Natalie Cassidy, Sonia from *EastEnders*, was a long game, as she only gets her schedule about a week in advance, so if I wanted her at my dinner table, I kind of had to just leave my diary open and pray. Eventually, one

Saturday morning, we had the nod. She drove herself over from Essex and promptly went to the wrong house entirely, about ten doors up the street. I found her looking slightly confused at my neighbour's house with a bottle of Pouilly-Fumé and a massive bag of beef crisps. Having her at my table talking about weight loss videos, Sunday lunches with her family and her time in stage school was wonderful. James May had to stop the interview every ten minutes for a rolled ciggie out on the back patio. He was delightful and had very strong views on how to arrange fish fingers in a white bread sandwich. We had to cut at least thirty minutes of his impassioned rants about why 'soup is not a meal' from the final interview.

I didn't plan for the interviews to be so weirdly emotional, but they seemed to dredge up feelings in both me and the guests that we had no idea we'd been bottling up. This was particularly true when I spoke to the musician Self Esteem over a cheese and white onion toasted sandwich (with salad cream for dipping). I'm reading her lyrics from 'I Do This All the Time' about not being jealous of other women and their wonderful lives, and suddenly I'm crying on my own podcast – properly crying! – and she has to give me a hug, and she's crying too.

Each guest has revealed something magical about themselves – and me.

The one thing I can never quite shake each time the celeb closes my front door is the urge to call home and share the gossip. To call the disconnected number that I know by heart and always will. Nobody will ever be as interested in what's going on in your life as your mother. And she'd have loved hearing about Rafe Spall in my living room talking about growing up around the cast of *Auf Wiedersehen, Pet*, or about how Stephen

Fry arrived with his mashed skippers and told me all about life with his husband, Elliott.

She'd have loved that I was keeping myself busy with *Comfort Eating*. 'There's no use sitting around with a face like lard,' she'd have said.

And there wasn't. So I did this instead.

The Golden Rules of
Comfort Eating

Over the course of this journey, a set of hazy rules has emerged over what is and what certainly isn't comfort food. They are devilishly difficult to lay down, because describing comfort eating very much involves phrases like 'just a feeling' or 'you know you when you know', and if you're being fancy you might say, 'I scatter a layer of Crunchy Nut cornflakes over tinned custard when I'm hungry as they add that certain *je ne sais quoi*.' But there definitely *are* rules: there's a distinct reason that I often namecheck the M&S food hall's Super Nutty Wholefood Salad as shorthand for 'not bloody comfort eating at all', then compare it with thickly buttered malt loaf, which seems to be universally understood as shorthand for a motherly arm around one's shoulder. When we're prepping podcast episodes, we sometimes reject our celebrities' first suggestions: things like laborious homemade beef Wellington, or dishes that require overnight marinades or ten different saucepans. It's just not what we do: we want to know what you eat when nobody's watching. One tedious, sulky, big-name star was taken off the schedule for demanding as his snack grilled steak and asparagus without any oil or butter. He had been difficult enough before he'd even got to my house, but this was the final straw. This healthy mix of lean protein and fresh veg, which we suspected he had prepared by a meal planner anyway, felt against the rules. So with that in mind, I should probably lay down the law:

A comfort food is a dish for one person. It's your special thing. It's basically YOU time in a bowl. Sure, you could be doing a ten-minute Hatha flow yoga stress release, or journalling about gratitude . . . but you can't say no to Warburtons giant crumpets with lemon curd.

You *might* cook your comfort food for two people at an absolute stretch. But you'd need to know the other person well. Or you're prepared to take that friendship to a new level by cooking them squeezy cheese and ham on toast with sweet chilli sauce for 'dinner'.

It's only a real comfort food if you blush and begin making excuses before revealing it to someone.

If you put it on Instagram, at least three people would slide into your DMs to say, 'U okay hun?'

If Gwyneth Paltrow had to eat your comfort food meal, she would cry more than when accepting the Academy Award for *Shakespeare in Love*.

Perishable ingredients are allowed, but frowned upon. Almost everything in your recipe could survive a nuclear incident. Just cockroaches, acid rain and a jar of Dorito dip.

All herbs must be dried and with long-ago sell-by dates, in tiny glass pots that have survived at least two house moves. No comfort food requires fresh tarragon.

Likewise, any food requiring a trip to a twice-monthly farmers' market is disqualified.

The big fancy black pepper grinder is permitted, and you are allowed to use so much of it that you find a piece behind your back tooth at four in the morning.

Extra points if you're using a brand that hasn't changed its box since 1967. You could use substitutions for said brand, but you know it won't be as good.

Your comfort food can be cooked in a microwave by simply pressing HIGH > 6 > START. No other buttons on the microwave must be touched.

A top-tier comfort eating recipe can, at a push, be assembled and eaten in a hotel room using only the implements provided: travel kettle, teaspoons, Corby trouser press.

It is acceptable for the dish to be delivered by dispatch rider, but extra points are given if weird changes need to be made (Tom Watson with his pitta-free kebab and Munya Chawawa with his Nando's pineapple and potato come to mind).

The food's main nutritional value is carbohydrate and fat. Protein comes last, and vitamins must be a mere suggestion and come in the form of ketchup; any comfort food containing high levels of vitamin K or magnesium is forbidden.

The food involves things that drip, stain and leave marks on your dressing gown, so you resemble something from Roald Dahl's *The Twits*.

Other people will find your comfort food repellent . . . and then they will love it after a few mouthfuls. Like my brother's blue cheese pizza. Until I met the dreamboat actor James Norton I did not know anchovies went with marmalade.

You have woken one morning to find the remnants of this food beside the sofa with the remote controls and a small blanket.

There is a story behind this dish that goes back decades. Either it is a veiled chance to recreate a dish your childminder made or it's something you cried yourself to sleep over at boarding school or something you learned to make and eat alone, because at the end of the day, who can you rely on but yourself? *No one.*

If you think this sounds a bit deep, then you clearly haven't heard *Comfort Eating*, because that's what I do. I invite you round, we eat Wotsits on toast and then we both cry.

Now, on with the show . . .

CHEESE

. . . And Why It Feels Like a Cuddle

Why does cheese feel like a cuddle? Well, it's because it just *does*. It's because an almost empty fridge containing a small slab of ageing Cheddar harbours at least a glimmer of hope – and even if that Cheddar has a tiny speck of mould, you can just scrape it off and turn a blind eye (I won't tell anyone). Find that toasty loaf you've got for emergencies in the bottom drawer of the fridge, add a dollop of something runny like brown sauce or some sort of chutney, and there you go: now you have dinner.

Cheese, in all its salty, fatty majesty, could well be the king of comfort foods. The top tier. I am always thrilled when a *Comfort Eating* guest – be it Rafe Spall, Self Esteem or Jaime Winstone – brings something cheesy. The interviews happen around lunchtime, by which point I'm often starving, and cheese is exactly what I want. Plus, interviewing people can be scary, and cheese is a great comforter. We have all at some point found ourselves standing in the light of the chiller cabinet, scooping grated red Leicester from the bag, head back, mouth open, pushing those slivers of loveliness down our throats and somehow feeling instantly better. And, in the same vein, after a hard day we have all leaned on that slightly fearsome chunk of apricot-laced Wensleydale which we panic-bought before Christmas before promptly forgetting about it – now, doesn't it taste good on cream crackers with a big cup of tea and

EastEnders? Suddenly your overdue car MOT seems marginally less upsetting.

I've thought about the transformative powers of cheese a lot over the years. Cows and farmers and dairy technicians and cheesemakers have perfected it, using techniques older than time to make something intense, pungent and sating that always hits the spot; they've done all the hard work, and now it's just sitting there in my fridge, available to me at any time. How does this magic happen? Why is it so unique to cheese? Why do some vegans – who have managed to dodge all other animal products – go on a lifelong quest to find the most pungent nut-based cheeses? And why do many would-be vegans name cheese as the one thing they cannot let go?

My theory about cheese is that it is special to British palates because it's so, well, completely *weird.* It's so unlike everything else we love, so unique both in flavour and in the sticky way it feels in our mouths. The British were never a nation who embraced stinky or slimy things, and we've never been ones for fermented nibbles or stuff covered with mildew or fungus. *Some* people have even called our food boring. Cheese, however, has always been the exception: a flirtation with the extremities of taste that we somehow took to our hearts. We may never show much passion for fermented bean curd, stinky herring or decaying vegetable stalks, but we will have a lovely, wobbly piece of whiffy Brie smeared on oatcakes. Cheese also has staying power; milky, fatty things linger in your mouth. They have a persistent aftertaste. You'll still know about that piece of Brie long after it has slipped down your gullet. It's still there as you get undressed and head for the toothbrush, and even in your dreams.

———

The cheapest Cheddar softening under a grill will always rico-
chet me back to autumn 1978, one of the saddest times of my
entire life. It's ten past midday in a living room in Currock, Carlisle. There's beige woodchip on the walls, a leather sofa with the
innards escaping and me, aged five, warming my chubby legs on
two bars of the gas fire. Mam tells me to move away from the
flame for the tenth time that week, in case my Holly Hobbie
nylon socks catch fire. As I warm my legs, the children's puppet
show *Pipkins* plays on our Grundig eighteen-inch telly in the
corner of the room. It's my favourite show, but right now it's
not cheering me up.

This is my first week at school, and needless to say I am not
a fan. I am making things very hard for my poor mother. The
Bishop Goodwin School is at the end of our street, only a few
hundred metres away, but still we've been late every day this
week. Every morning my face is a vision of indignation and
snot, and she drags me in, apologetic and upset that I'm showing her up like this. And even though, as the days have gone on,
I've begun to rather enjoy the plot of *The Enormous Turnip*,
which my class reads each morning after register, I'm still kick-
ing and screaming every time.

'Be a big girl,' she tells me.

My problem with this 'school' thing is that I liked the previous
arrangement far more. I *loved* those long, dreamy summer days
that me and Mam spent together with my brother David in his
pram. A whole day spent going to Woolworths on a mission to
buy darning wool, then a trip to the library at Tullie House to take
back Grandad's latest detective book, followed by a glass of banana
Nesquik in a tearoom, sharing a pink iced bun sprinkled with hun-
dreds and thousands; or just afternoons spent at home with Mam

making rock cakes as I watched *Fingerbobs* or played with my pop-up treehouse, or her putting hems on skirts and sewing up holes in socks while we watched *Crown Court* on Border TV.

But now it's September and apparently I'm a big girl, and every day I'm to be whisked up that street by one arm, cold north winds biting my knees and my black rubber galoshes nipping my heels as we go. Once there I am cruelly abandoned – or so it seems. Mam swears she watches me through the window for at least ten minutes. She says she sees me on the classroom floor sitting cross-legged joining in with the 'Okki Tokki Unga' song, which is actually a lot of fun (not that I'd be admitting this). Years later, Mam told me she'd wander home at 9.15 a.m., close the front door, sit down on the sofa and cry for most of the three hours until she picked me up for lunch.

'Here she is, Lizzy Tish,' Mam would say as I appeared through the school gates at lunchtime to walk the few short steps home. We lived so close she said it felt daft paying for school dinner. Besides, she'd seen what Carlisle Council was serving up: cold hot dogs and thrice-warmed-up carrots. She knew she could do better. I needed food that made me smile. Hand in hand, we walked home while I regaled her with tales about stolen Stickle Bricks, Robin Hood or, of course, adventures which featured Our Lord Jesus Christ. He featured a lot at my Church of England school. Water to wine, feeding the five thousand with a few fishes and a loaf – you name it, Big JC could do it.

'So you liked school better today?'

'No,' I said, angling for an afternoon on the couch watching *The Sullivans*, inhaling her Oil of Ulay moisturiser. Mam had the gas fire on, waiting. I toasted my scabbed knees as she disappeared into the kitchen. There was some banging of drawers and cupboards in the kitchen. Then the aroma of Cheddar heating, liquefying, then browning, filled the living room. I slumped down into Dad's big tweed-covered chair with the bits of chewing gum tangled in the arms. House rules decreed that I could sit in this chair until 5.40 p.m. when Dad came home from work. Right now, I had free rein to snuggle in and watch Hartley Hare from *Pipkins* – a scraggy puppet with floppy and demonic habits who I adored. And then Mam appeared, carrying the most delicious thing in her entire cooking repertoire: Mam's cheese on toast.

Just the sight of the plate appearing cosied away a little of my discombobulation. She'd taken two slices of Mother's Pride from the white crinkly packet – it's that plasticky, square sort we're made to feel sheepish about buying in the modern day, despite it being oh so delicious. The bread was grilled on one side until golden, then buttered on the other, before thick slices of Cheddar were laid on top. Then it was toasted until the visible crusts were *almost* burned, and the cheese was crisp but still wobbly enough that my little teeth left prints in it as I bit, cheese threads oozing from my mouth and back onto the plate. Melted cheese is truly unadulterated joy.

On the Friday of that first week, the weather turned cold and she brought me half a mug of warm Campbell's cream of tomato soup: something sweet, silky and vividly orange to go with my usual order. She transferred it in a tray to my lap, with a warning not to get my cuffs in the ketchup or the soup, before leaving me as the screen danced with Bungle the bear and George the pink dragon. Happiness restored. I toddled off back to school that afternoon, not exactly pleased to be going but certainly more affable than I was that morning.

The cheese I ate in my childhood lacked variety. It certainly lacked glamour, too. It would be a long road until I found myself eating fancy French reblochon or Swedish Västerbotten or any other of those cheeses you might see on a board in a fancy gastropub, accompanied by some of those black, tasteless charcoal wafers that mean you're somewhere posh. In the eighties my family only ever ate Cheddar, or, if we were branching out, red Leicester. Maybe Gran had the smallest chunk of Stilton at Christmas. We knew nothing better and we never got bored. Forty years later, I am still not bored by Cheddar.

Neither can I ever be sniffy about heavily processed cheese, like the stuff that comes in squares wrapped in plastic, or the squeezy stuff in metal tubes. To me this is the taste of the summer holidays of my childhood. I so vividly remember opening the fridge door and finding Kraft Singles, feeling as though I had hit the jackpot – they were so perfect for sneaking up your sleeve, with an extra one for your mate, and then eating down on the old abandoned allotments, or wherever we'd made our latest den. Or the Primula cheese and chive that I squeezed onto Ritz crackers when Mam was watching *Dynasty* with Joan Collins on Friday nights – so very satisfying, so very chic.

And that's not to mention 'spready cheese', which to my mind is a vastly underrated pleasure, one far too déclassé to ever be cited in 'proper' food writing. A Dairylea cheese triangle, released from its foil and then sucked from the silver while watching Noel Edmonds on *Multi-Coloured Swap Shop*, was one of my fledgling food critic experiences. Eating that squidgy, semi-liquefied, factory-refined cheese goo takes the eater almost to the very limits of 'ick'. It leapfrogs decadent and plants its boots firmly in wanton. And yet somehow it's bloody delicious.

My father, however, always had aspirations. He was a Scouser, held hostage by fortune in Carlisle, but this didn't stop him behaving like an international man of mystery. He had dark skin but claimed his family was Irish and sometimes sported a Burt Reynolds-style moustache. He also claimed to be able to speak German, although he only really knew a few words, like *sehr gut* and *Liebfraumilch*, learned while stationed in Hamburg in the army. And he once won a load of money on the horses in the eighties and promptly bought a clapped-out Jaguar, consumed by rust, which he thought made us look like yuppies but really made us look like drug dealers on all our trips to Fine Fare (the bottom eventually fell out and it was taken for scrap).

It perhaps isn't a surprise then that my Dad was responsible for the first exotic turn in my cheese journey. In the mid-eighties a local supermarket called Walter Willson began stocking Bavarian smoked cheese, which he remembered from his time spent in Germany. He popped it in the basket and from then on Mam bought him it as a treat. This cheese came in an actual shape, and it had a brown plastic cover – unheard of! It was creamy and smoky and irresistible. Me and my brother drove Dad mad by taking it from the fridge and eating it with a knife while watching *The Fall Guy* and *Blockbusters* with Bob Holness. Dad's special cheese and Dad's special chair were certainly treated with decreasing reverence as we turned into sneering teens. I still buy that Bavarian cheese, but nowadays in pre-packed round slices from M&S, which is perfect for literally posting into your mouth like a love letter to yourself at the end of a horrible day.

While my Dad may have won us round to experiencing Germany, though, he certainly didn't have any love for France. It was the nineties, almost a decade on, before we bought anything from that far-flung land, and goodness me did we miss out. All sticky, stinky, soft-rinded French cheeses are the epitome of comfort eating. Have you ever baked a Brie and then scooped soft bread through its wobbly innards? Or hurled chunks of Camembert into a deep-fat fryer and served it with bramble jam? It is ecstasy.

But for so long the Dents simply did not 'do France'. Like many Northern working-class Brits in the nineties, we found France a rather unsettling and unknowable place. No one we knew ever went on holiday there, aside from our doctor, who spent three weeks each summer in a tent in Brittany, which we thought sounded like hell. Apparently the locals insisted on speaking French to him the whole time. The only person I knew who went was my friend's dad Ronnie, who had a transit van. Sometimes he used to drive to Boulogne on a day trip to stock up on Rothmans fags and cut-price frizzante, and when he got back he'd be greeted like Phileas Fogg.

So, France: we didn't trust it, and we didn't trust the Brie which they had started stocking in our flashy new Asda on Junction 44 of the M6, which opened in 1987, turning our gastronomical lives upside down. For a start, this Brie didn't act like normal cheese. It wasn't stiff and it wasn't even orange. It was, instead, pale and gelatinous. It was a bit sweaty, and even a bit wobbly. And it had a skin on it that none of us knew if we could eat without it killing us, and we couldn't even check: the instructions were in foreign.

I can still remember the breakthrough, though: a TV advert for a French soft cheese called Boursin. It began playing in every ad break, showing close-up shots of creamy garlicky cheesy pulp, encrusted with dried herbs. The French folk on the ads would lap it up on bread with a glass of wine – '*Du pain, du vin, du Boursin*', went the catchphrase. It was all so sophisticated. Yes, Boursin was made by Unilever, probably in an industrial park in Hounslow, and yes, it left you with breath so lively it might get you kicked off public transport, but our horizons were suddenly so much wider. Sometimes me and my brother would grab piles of Mighty White and eat it with Boursin while watching *Airwolf*, our constant sibling war of dead arms and name-calling temporarily suspended. Peace breaking out over the Bavarian smoky and Boursin, knifed straight from the wrapper and plopped in our mouths.

When I have those cheeses now, it reminds me that those truly were some of the happiest times of my life, especially considering that it wasn't long after that I was moving out and starting to fend for myself.

In the early nineties, I moved to Stirling in Scotland, to study English literature. Aged eighteen I saw Carlisle and my Mam's house as a prison, but soon enough I realised that I'd kill to grump moodily up our back lane wearing a Smiths T-shirt, fractal leggings and baseball boots, juggling files of A-level history papers while letting myself in, heading for the fridge, swinging open the door to find it heaving with reduced-sticker treasure.

My Mam's Jenga-style fridge arrangements were legendary among my friends: bags of grated mozzarella (reduced to thirty-two pence) sat on coleslaw (WHOOPS! Forty-two pence), and together they rested on cream buns (SPECIAL OFFER: 8 FOR

THE PRICE OF 6) beside eight litres of full-fat milk which had to be drunk by tomorrow. There was a running joke that my Mam was always panic buying for an apocalypse that only she knew about, as she had a hotline to the Number 10 war cabinet. More accurately, though, she simply loved the big new exciting supermarkets springing up all around the edges of Carlisle, with their midnight shopping and endless aisles of plenty. And she *loved* feeding. She loved those days when our house was a stop-off point for a revolving cast of at least thirty teenagers, pulling up in Ford Escorts and banged-up Renault Clios, all the boys with long curtains wearing Ton Sur Ton and Chipie, eating her bacon sandwiches and double fried egg sandwiches on white bloomer rolls. No one ever went hungry at Mam's house.

And then, all of a sudden, I was a student. I rapidly learned that those 'quick student meals for a quid' books which parents packed their children off to college with were really very little use. I was never going to soak mung beans overnight or make my own pesto, and boiling brown rice for thirty-five minutes always felt like far too much of a life commitment. I was sharing a small, sparse kitchen in university halls with ten people, and any food would have to be eaten while sitting on the edge of a single bed in a twelve-by-eight-foot breezeblock-walled room.

I missed my mother and her cooking very much, although I was never going to admit this, as I was now a fully grown adult who didn't need any of that: I was far too busy reading Virginia Woolf novels, snogging boys with pierced nipples and listening to Edie Brickell. Each week my Mam would send a handwritten letter containing Carlisle news along with a BT phonecard in the hope that it would prod me to walk the full fifty metres from my bed to the payphone and give them a call. God, they're so demanding, I thought. Jesus, I was an idiot. Sometimes I wish I could time travel simply to punch myself in the face.

Fear not, though, for I shall call these years: The Cheese Years. Cheese was my saviour. For instance: take an anaemic twenty-four-hour Esso garage frozen pizza bought on the way home from the Fubar nightclub in Stirling, scatter a handful of cheap Lancashire crumbly on top, add a pinch of mixed herbs if you can steal some from Helga from Norway's cupboard, along with a scooch of black pepper, and suddenly you have a feast. Or sling a layer of Edam onto a Findus beefburger, melt it, then slather mayo across the bun, and you've got something quite delicious. Best of all was the uni canteen, deep in the bowels of the Macrobert Centre, where large stodgy bowls of macaroni cheese were twenty-two pence – these would be eaten while moaning to your friends about that boy you snogged at the 'Balls Up' juggling party and how he didn't leave a written message on your uni room door asking you out. Even if dating before phones proved to be arduous, the filling, sating, comforting power of cheese never lost its strength.

In my second year I was turfed out of the university halls and into the town. It was at this point that things got rather desperate: I lived miles from the canteen, and due to some, ahem, budgeting issues, I had already spent most of my student loan on Rolling Rock beer and feather boas in order to look like Lady Miss Kier from Deee-Lite (reader, I didn't look remotely like her). Quite frankly, I was skint and looking for a way out, and that way out happened to be Iceland.

No, not the magical Nordic country, but Iceland frozen foods on Stirling High Street, which sold a Stranraer-made cheese called 'Seriously Strong Cheddar' at slashed prices. It's important to note that this cheese never came in small packs of, say, 200 grams. No, it was only the gargantuan one-kilo blocks. These clonking landmasses of cheese went for around forty pence. Putting on my best Loyd Grossman voice, I would stand in a grotty student kitchen, with its sink full of dishes and posters of hunky Gary Speed from Leeds United pinned to the fridge, making my friends laugh by 'pairing' it with Iceland's twelve-for-the-price-of-four crumpets. Sometimes I would bake the whole thing in a tray with a breadcrumb or porridge-oat topping and call it 'Iceland crumpets *au gratin*', or I'd simply cut slices of the cheese and eat it with lemon curd, or whatever else was sweet and nine pence a jar – this was often done at 2 a.m. while trying to speed read H. G. Wells's *The Island of Dr Moreau* for a 9 a.m. tutorial.

If none of this sounds very posh, or befitting of an eminent food writer, you are exactly right. Yes, in recent times the middle classes have embraced cheaper supermarkets such as Aldi and Lidl, whipping in and out at off-peak times to load up on ricotta for £1.29 a tub while wearing pulled-down hats and dark glasses to avoid being recognised by someone from their choral group. Iceland, however, they will not touch. Iceland will always be too common.

And lo and behold, I'd soon find myself in fancy London where things were going to get even stickier in this regard.

Cheese does not *have* to be expensive. Yes, fancy Stilton is what people talk about in posh food magazines, but deep down we all know the restorative properties of a bag of Babybels. Hooray for peeling the red wax off those tiny spheres of happiness as the bus trundles home from a terrible date, popping them into your mouth whole, gob open like an upright anaconda. And three cheers for adding a large dollop of pale sticky Dairylea to buttered pasta. No, you won't see this on cookery shows, but you're behind closed doors now. You're eating like nobody's watching. This is self-care 101.

It was only when I began mixing with more 'worldly' people in London, however, that I understood the significance of cheese to the posh. We are all, at some level, cheese obsessives, or 'turophiles' as they might say. If you have ever seen the queues at cheese stalls at the city's Borough Market on a Saturday morning, you'll know that they are full of men called Rufus who were sent to board at Ludgrove aged eight and had mothers who loved the labradors more than them. The posh might not be big on physical hugging and affection, but if a Rufus rises at 5 a.m. to source you a truffled Baron Bigod or a rich, oozing Tunworth, well, you know you're high in their esteem.

Beginning my career in media in 1996 certainly opened my eyes to how unposh I was, with my silver fillings, dropped Ts, Kookaï bootcut trousers and lack of conversational Latin. This got to me so much that I began adding my middle name to my byline in *Marie Claire* to make me sound more glamorous: I was Grace *Georgina* Dent, not regular Grace Dent. The name Grace Dent, I thought, was two short grunts, a bit like being barked at by a pitbull with kennel cough. Grace Georgina Dent, on the other hand, sounds like she's summered in Martha's Vineyard, can get out of an Aston Martin without flashing her pant elastic and, most importantly, knows her way round a cheeseboard when posh folk are in the vicinity.

I can clearly recall my first trip, at the age of twenty-six, to a country house in Suffolk where the hosts served cheeses (please note: posh people pluralise cheese as 'cheeses'). Eating cheese in front of people with trust funds and names like Blaise and Romulus is nerve-wracking, and realising that the Dent family had lived all this time without our own 'cheese cave' was humbling. No, I didn't know these existed, either. A cheese cave is a very cold room underneath one's Grade II listed former Elizabethan monastery country retreat where the posh store precious things that need a specific ambience: spaniel kibble, artillery for their blunderbusses and, of course, Stilton. I learned that by serving cheeses at room temperature, their stinky richness is ramped up to the max, and all the fattiness comes into its own. The flavours in cold cheese are all tangled up and stunted; good cheese needs to be removed from your cave at least three hours pre-dinner party, which is about the time when I start sticking Cheddar cubes on cocktail sticks to make a cheese and pineapple porcupine – but that's just me.

Anyway. In this grand house, I'm sitting in front of an enormous board filled with strange oddities and one of the other guests asks for a 'cheese harp', which I'm told is used to cut the Comté and not to perform an impromptu version of 'Wonderwall'. Someone else is brandishing a limited-edition Fortnum & Mason silver-plated cheese fork, which I don't like the look of. I decide to pick up a knife and tread precariously towards something that resembles a Cheddar, helping myself to the lovely pointy end bit. This is, in fact, a grave error. You *never* cut the 'nose' off the cheese. Posh people get tremendously agitated about this. They believe that something round like a Brie should be served in slices, like a cake, so everyone gets a little bit of the middle and some of the rind. Also, if anything has got blue veins in it then good luck, as one needs to slice it so that everyone can get a little of the pungent mould. Yes, you are expected to basically divide up something that already looks like an Ordnance Survey map so that everyone at the table gets a little of the most lush territories. Oh, and yes, you can eat the rind. But only if it's younger than twenty-four months. And you should never eat the rind if the cheese is wrapped in bark, like I did, unless you want someone doing the Heimlich manoeuvre while other men stand around frowning about the British comprehensive system.

Regardless, despite all the secret rules and fancy instruments, I'm very glad to say that the familiar sense of cheese-fug happiness did set in. There you have it. Cheese is the great leveller, uniting people from across the social classes. Until I asked for some Branston pickle and a maybe a couple of Tuc crackers. I was never asked back.

My father, who as you remember spoke fluent German,* had various Teutonic-style nicknames for my mother. 'Mein Führer' was his favoured one, which came up any time Mam was laying down the odds about his half-done DIY jobs, his inability to pay any bill until the angry red one arrived, or his hogging of the TV remote to play endless episodes of *Inspector Morse*. In conversation, he would refer to her as 'She Who Must Be Obeyed'. He'd say this in the manner of Herr Flick from the

---

* He spoke approximately thirty-five words of German: ten of them were beer brands and one was the word for potato salad.

BBC comedy *'Allo 'Allo*, indicating that my mother's wishes were sacrosanct in this house, and if she wished us all to be up at 8 a.m. to catch the Allied Carpets bank holiday sale then we were probably, for a quieter life, doing it.

Dad lived in Germany with the army in the fifties and again in the sixties, not too long after the Second World War, and when he spoke about it he'd talk glowingly of the breakfast, or *Frühstück*. There would be groaning tables of bread rolls, ten types of jam, some butter and honey, boiled eggs, fruits and, of course, cheese. It must have felt very different from his life in Liverpool.

When I was small, maybe three or four, I can remember him making Mam cheese and jam on toast, a quirk he'd picked up in Düsseldorf. I imagine it was something they roughly cobbled together in an army barracks before running out of the door. Dad had about four recipes in his entire repertoire and Mam loved this one: thick slabs of Cheddar on buttered toast with a thick layer of some of Gran's bramble jam. We had an endless supply of this bramble jam as Gran made it in huge batches and kept it in the airing cupboard.

My parents were not a massively lovey-dovey couple. Public displays of affection were unthinkable. I can still hear them in peals of laughter in our kitchen in the seventies as they'd seen a married couple they knew holding hands in the street as they walked along to town. My parents had spotted them from their car and could hardly contain their mirth. Holding hands! Normal folk just didn't act like that.

But despite bickering almost every day for the best part of forty-five years, and despite the fact they spent their evenings in front of the telly sitting on different sofas, never cuddled up together, I knew they were passionately in love – even if she cried much more over our cat Sooty dying of old age than over any of the times Dad threatened to leave. She knew he'd always come back. He couldn't live without her. She was the one who sorted out his tax discs and bought his socks, after all.

'Take this to the German,' he would say, as I passed him one day in the eighties, thrusting into my hands her special Silver Jubilee mug filled with white tea and a cheese and jam toasted sandwich for her. 'The German'. Another of his nicknames. Really, that is all a long-term relationship is: perseverance, companionship, nicknames and in-jokes. I would transport the cheesy jammy sandwich from his hands by the toaster to her on the sofa, with a message from him:

'Dad says he loves you very much,' I'd say.

'*Pshhht*. He must be after something.'

Sometimes I try to pinpoint the very last time they set eyes on each other. It is so muddled in my head: an overgrown forest filled with care homes in lockdown, cancer appointments, the rot of dementia and goodbyes that never mattered to him as he didn't even know she'd been there. There was no great goodbye, just a fizzling out and half a year of no contact at all.

In the last weeks of her life, I made her a cheese and pickle sandwich, in the dark, exhausted by sleepless nights. This was one of the only 'proper' meal things I could still feed her. I cut the sandwich into four small squares like you'd feed a child, and sat on the edge of the hospital bed the council had delivered. I passed her the sandwich. She took a small bite and swallowed. Then another.

'Cheese and pickle,' I said.

'Yes.'

'You don't have to eat all of it.'

'I like it.' We sat in silence. 'This isn't pickle,' she whispered.

'Yes it is,' I said, scrunching up my nose. She carried on chewing and swallowed.

'This is jam,' she replied. I picked up the sandwich and sniffed it. I thought it must be the drugs talking, but when I held it up to a chink of light coming through the curtains from a streetlight, I knew she was absolutely right. She was in fact holding a Cheddar and jam sandwich. In my haze of tiredness, I'd mixed up the jars.

She ate a little more of the sandwich before passing me the plate and closing her eyes.

'Just like Dad used to make,' I said.

'Yes, for the German.'

'For the German.' Wherever he was, he was still with her.

Scarlett Moffatt's

Beans on Toast
with Crushed Wotsits

I adored interviewing Scarlett Moffatt, especially as she was kind enough to invite me to her home in the North-East. My producers and I took a train to Newcastle before driving a hire car miles and miles into remote Northumberland, where villages trailed off into picturesque nothingness. Doing *Comfort Eating* like this was unique. Most of the episodes take place in my house, giving the interviews a very specific feel: this is my little place where I have lived for years, with all my books and ornaments and family photos and cats running about, coughing up furballs. I am completely exposed, and no matter how many times I dash around hiding council tax bills and making sure there's nothing covered in fungus in the fridge, the celeb will arrive and I'll notice a pair of my partner's boxer shorts randomly drying on a radiator.

So when Scarlett Moffatt said, 'Why don't you come to my house?', I just couldn't resist – not only because she's thoroughly delightful, but also because the nosy part of me wanted to see the sort of house that piles of *I'm a Celebrity . . . Get Me Out of Here* cash can get you. From the moment the door opened, she was adorable: warm, open, dishing out cups of tea and being completely candid about her ascent from 'lass next door who ended up on *Gogglebox*' to 'famous person trying to live a London celeb lifestyle'. She made Camden her home after she shot to fame, but Scarlett felt desperately lonely in the heaving, dirty city. Soon enough she headed back north to be near her family and close group of schoolfriends. I empathised entirely with this. For most people who leave small towns for a big city, there's a sort of emotional magnetic force dragging them back. It never quite leaves, even decades later, that urge to be back in a living room with people who understand what you mean before you've even finished your sentence.

Scarlett's comfort food absolutely understood the brief: beans on toast with a cheese Wotsit topping. Perfection. She did not attempt to gild the lily or hide her strange peccadilloes from the public eye. Here you have the taste of cheesy beans on toast but without the arduous stage of turning the grill on and melting cheese over the beans. Oh no, just coat the top of the beans with a thick carpet of crushed Wotsit dust, and *voilà*. *C'est formidable.*

Scarlett's embarrassment was real as she revealed it; the best *Comfort Eating* snacks always begin with the guest cringing and trying to backtrack as they whip the tea towel off the tray to reveal the slapdash 'feast'. She first began making it at university in York, where she fondly remembers being out almost every night partying, leaving few pennies for such frivolities as 'groceries'. Vital supplies like vodka, self-tan and stick-on eyelashes had to be bought instead. 'And cheese is so expensive!' she told me as she scrunched the Wotsits over the plate – it still makes me laugh now, as she was standing in a bespoke white marble dream kitchen which I remember gave me distinct life envy.

She admitted that she still makes this snack whenever she has a night in front of the telly. I loved the idea that there was a place in Scarlett's heart that would always find cheese an expensive purchase, and also how her special comfort food was rooted in those student days when life was so simple: party, sleep, get up, eat beans on toast with Wotsits, repeat. Time and again our comfort foods are a root back to a moment in time when we were truly happy: that sandwich that saved our life, that chocolate bar that got us through the break-up, those beans on toast with Wotsits that kept you alive when you'd spent your weekly budget on two-for-one Smirnoff Ices.

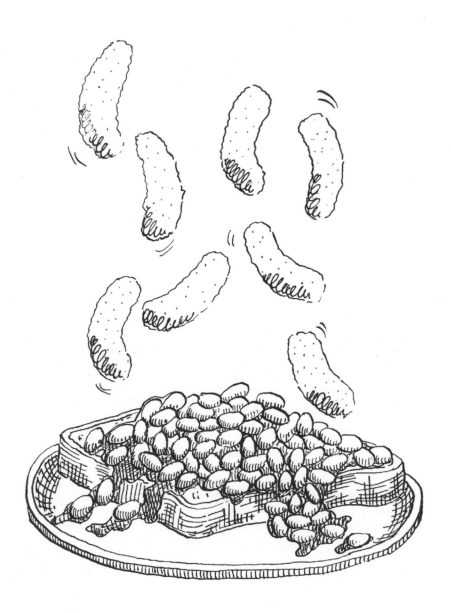

THE RECIPE

---

2 slices white bread
Butter
Baked beans
Wotsits
The recklessness of youth

Go to student night. Dance to 'We Found Love' by Rihanna while imbibing several shots of a shoddily launched liquor that the breweries are palming off on students. It tastes like apricot and feet, but they're selling two shots for fifty pence.

Leave nightclub, realise feet really hurt in Top Shop kitten heels. Take off shoes and walk last 500 metres to taxi rank despite real and present risk of catching tetanus.

Return to student flat, stepping over traffic cone, various tree branches and garden gnomes that fellow students have found incredibly funny to bring home.

Attend to crying flatmate Florence, who is distraught because even though Steve's been back at this flat three times in the last month he has gone home from the club with Iggy and 'it's jushttt disrespectful'. Listen for twenty-five minutes until she passes out.

Begin making post-club snack. Try to clear a surface as no one has tidied the kitchen for seven days. Is the thing in the sink part of Tabby's art project or is it just the grill pan with Cif in it? Hard to tell.

Find baked beans. Realise you do not possess any bread, cheese or Wotsits. Why does this cupboard not replenish itself like the one at Mum's house? Why is being an adult so relentlessly chore-filled and 'listy'?

Steal ingredients from flatmates' cupboards. It's not stealing if you intend to replace it all. Take bread from Tabby's freezer drawer. 'Borrow' Wotsits from beneath flatmate Luke's bed where he keeps his stash of delicious things that his mum sends him. Ignore all other things under his bed. It's for the best.

Toast bread. Turn dial on toaster right up to highest level as you are very hungry and cannot possibly wait. You are in fact so close to starvation that you can feel your body breaking down and ingesting its own internal organs.

Open beans. Look for clean bowl to microwave them in. Give up. Look for mug. Give up. Place beans in old Gold Blend coffee jar waiting to go to recycling. Microwave.

Check phone. Become distracted by scrolling clips of kittens being found and rescued from bushes. Forget about toast. Smell toast beginning to burn. Press eject button. Scrape toast over sink, showering art project and yourself with black, charred carbon.

Spread toast with butter, or whatever spread available. Right to the corners of the bread.

Pour beans out of jar onto toast.

Take packet of Wotsits and scrunch up until they go from being orange, fully formed 'worm' shapes to crunchy, cheesy dust.

Festoon the Wotsits over the beans on toast, so they set like a delicious carpet of maize, rapeseed oil and flavour enhancer disodium 5-ribonucleotide.

Amble as fast as you can with blisters to your bedroom, before other flatmates return home and begin questioning the provenance of your ingredients.

Get into bed, remove false eyelashes. Place on bedside table with four other pairs and many, many dried contact lenses.

Eat delicious cheese–bean–bread amalgam. Feel instantly cosy, full and content. Feel additionally smug that you didn't give any money to Mr Pizza King on the High Road. Finish by wiping last piece of crust around the plate, soaking up the last of the bean sauce.

Place plate on floor. You'll take it to the kitchen tomorrow. With all the mugs.

Feel sleepy. Pull up duvet around you.

Fall asleep in dress, again. Happy.

The Inaugural
Comfort Eating Honours

During my inevitable reign, the following people will receive instant *Comfort Eating* honours:

Aunt Bessie – OBE

The nation's imaginary nan and the saviour of those hangovers when you only have a vague memory of promising several friends in the pub a 'Sunday lunch', Aunt Bessie is the diligent human you are not. Thank heavens for her roasties, Yorkshire puds and parsnips. This entire brand is laziness rebadged as love, and it works.

We all love Bessie. She's the sort of twinkly-eyed, caring nan who's been up since 7 a.m., taken herself to church for communion and a gossip, and had time to shove a hoover around her front room, one of those 'hoovers' that's just a box on a stick that makes a HDDDDDDD sound. She's had time to tinker with boiling pans, too, because Aunt Bessie *cares*. She wants you to get a proper meal across your chest. She takes up the slack. She knows the old-school cooking tips you probably didn't learn, you with your fancy ideas about 'a career'. Do you know how the cheese sauce sticks to the cauliflower? Don't worry, Bessie does.

Mr Kipling – OBE

The absolute don of British teatimes, making exceedingly good cakes since 1967. Or at least brightly packaged, convenient cakes. *The Great British Bake Off* this is not, but is there anything more cheering than a pot of tea and a box of fondant French Fancies? Can the rattle of a box of Unicorn Slices fail to spark joy? The man turned the Bakewell tart and the Battenberg cake into something portable, and not just a thing you saw in the fancy tea shop you got taken to once a year by Gran.

When I was a child, his Farmhouse Cake was a favourite: sweet, moist, beige and slightly stodgy with big fat sultanas. Sure, it was made in a factory, but it had a definite rustic feel. Nowadays Mr Kipling marks the seasons changing with Easter egg cakes, Halloween orange chocolate slices and a festive Bakewell. And yes, his Hot Cross Pies are just the Christmas mince pies with a different packet, but let's not nitpick.

Bill O'Brien and Harry Norville, inventors of the Breville – MBE

Two Australians with one big dream and a huge legacy. The Breville toastie machine has brought more joy into my life than all the winners of the Booker Prize for literature put together. Everyone in my class in 1985 had at least one Breville battle scar from hastily retrieving a tuna melt while trying to rush back to *Smokey and the Bandit* on VHS.

A baked bean and cheese Breville with a salad cream puddle was the summer holiday brunch food of champions. You need to overfill the Breville just enough so that the beans and cheese seep out of the sides, and the bread must be buttered on the outside. The magic is in the waiting. Do not open that machine too early! (Important: after plating up, wait a little, as the innards are hotter than Venus.)

Captain Birdseye – Distinguished Conduct Medal

Swashbuckling, bearded king of the high seas and the chiller cabinet, the Captain has been over-excited about haddock fish fingers my entire life. Captain Birdseye and his ship of hyperactive children nagged us to nag our mothers. We didn't want the cheap supermarket brand fish fingers which he told us were full of 'grey bits': we wanted these fancy ones in the bright yellow boxes made by the man with the big ship full of happy shipmates!

I loved Captain Birdseye because not only was he unashamedly shady about all his competitors, but he also had the snowiest, fluffiest beard and his own maritime currency, 'Birdseye Lucky Coins'. This salty sea dog – played by John Hewer, then Thomas Pescod – seemed like a very old man when I was a little girl, so it was a worrying time in my life when I began having the hots for the silver seagoing hunk-of-stuff Riccardo Acerbi who played him from 2018. I can only imagine this is what happens when you let perimenopausal women do the casting. They'd have greenlit him before he'd even got his waders on.

The Ferrero Rocher ambassador – the Most Distinguished Order of St Michael and St George for Services to the Carlisle Community

Was there anything more exciting in the nineties than getting a glimpse inside the ambassador's reception in that Ferrero Rocher advert? Men in smart suits and women with sharp bobs and power shoulder pads enjoyed the ambassador's 'exquisite taste that always captivates his guests' – aka the massive pile of Ferrero Rocher chocolates served by a butler on a silver platter. For many of us, this was one of the fanciest gatherings we'd ever seen – now we knew what posh folk ate behind closed doors! Thank you, ambassador, for letting me dream about what life would be like when I eventually married Prince Albert of Monaco!

Ferrero Rocher may have become a bit of a joke over the years, but the sight of that plastic box with the flip-open lid full of gold wrappers in their brown paper baskets still makes my heart do a loop-the-loop. They're still delicious: the perfect bullet of cheap praline and whole hazelnuts wrapped in chocolate. When I eat one it's Christmas 1991 all over again: I'm listening to 'Fairground' by Simply Red and arguing with my brother David over who gets the last one. Bliss.

BUTTER

. . . And Why It Seems to Make Everything Just That Little Bit Better

We are hard-wired to love butter. It's in our collective DNA. Twinkling. Yearning. A feeling older than time, older than all of us. You'll feel it in longing for a silky-smooth, fluffy, all-butter croissant, the butter creating those light pockets of air that make it so very sumptuous. You'll feel it when you spot that pain au chocolat in the window of the bakery on a Saturday morning, the one that leaves a buttery smear as it's lifted from parchment paper. It's there in the butter spread thickly by the nice lady with capable hands in the takeaway sandwich bar at ten past midday, when your email inbox is full and you're already dreaming of getting back into your pyjamas. All of this butter feels like an act of care.

There is literally no dish in culinary existence that will not be improved by twenty-five grams of butter being tossed in with wilful abandon. I dare you to try and prove me wrong. Butter is a sweetener, it is a softener, it is the culinary version of italics saying *and now we're a little bit fancy*. Butter is home, but it's home when you've put the hoover round and plumped up the cushions. Butter is a hand on your shoulder saying, 'Take a breath. Things are hard, yes, but for this moment in time, you're fine.' No wonder we love it so much.

Real butter is what *Comfort Eating* guests always use in their snacks. It was oceans of Kerrygold oozing down the sides of Aisling Bea's potato waffles and spaghetti hoop stack; good salted grass-fed French organic butter that Rafe Spall spread like tarmac on his Cathedral City Cheddar sandwich; and the stuff smothered liberally along the bottom of Jay Blades's bun and cheese. The Danes call this exuberance *tandsmør*, meaning 'tooth butter': butter spread so thickly you leave teeth marks as you chomp. It's something I aspire to.

No guest on *Comfort Eating* ever asks for margarine. When people really want to be comforted, they go for the good stuff. The stuff you get in crisp, folded packets that open elegantly, a fresh pat of which instantly makes one feel brighter. Not butter substitute, and never anything in a yellow plastic box with a name like 'Crikey O'Reilly This Tastes Like the Real Thing' or 'Notterly Butterly but Pretty Damn Close'. Marge – even the name is dowdy – has played a huge part in my eating journey, but let's be honest: it rarely sparks joy . . . does it?

At my house, one of my proudest possessions is a turquoise Le Creuset butter dish that lives by the toaster, always bearing room-temperature salted butter. Yes, let me clang the name Le Creuset with its classy, chunky practicality and reassuringly expensive price tag. All Generation X working-class women love Le Creuset because it reminds us of that one posh friend's mother who read *Good Housekeeping* and did a Friday night soufflé. John Lewis's Le Creuset section is like catnip to upwardly mobile Aga-chasers like me. When worldwide nuclear armageddon inevitably kicks off, I will walk calmly to the aisle with those 1.9 litre-capacity heart-shaped dishes. It's my safe space.

I love my butter dish for many reasons. For one, I've had it for ten years without smashing off the handle, thus marking a period of my life when I've been mature enough to 'have a nice thing' without breaking it while moving house, losing it in a hotel room or having it stolen during a house party by someone who also smashed the toilet seat. Let's call this stage of my life, for want of argument, 'middle age'. Becoming middle-aged has several downsides, but one terrific thing is that I am now the sort of organised, upright adult who can at any time whip the lid off my earthenware butter dish and find something magical to slather across hot toasted crumpets. Or pikelets. Or drop scones. Or Scotch pancakes. Or any of those other absurdly delicious batter-based items with shifting regional definitions that can swiftly cause a pub argument. I cannot in good faith tell you where a griddle scone finishes and an English muffin begins, but I do know they offer roughly the same amount of comfort as the butter seeps into their creases, melds with their crispy bottoms and runs down your chin as you bite into them.

The main reason I love my butter dish, though, is because loving butter and using it freely as a comfort food has been a very long road for me. For almost all my life, from round about 1978, we didn't eat butter chez Dent – and I know exactly why.

Butter has been especially prevalent in my family tree. My grandmother and her ancestors were a gnarly, can-do bunch who lived in remote north Cumberland in the 'Debatable Lands' around the Anglo–Scottish border. These lands were termed thus because for a long time it was debatable whether they were Scottish or English, and this came with a considerable amount of bloodshed and general cross-border umbrage.

For centuries my family ate little else but bread, turnips and a little meat. By God, their diets were slender of choice. I heard tales of my Gran loading an old suitcase with bread crusts, then walking for miles to a chicken farmer to barter for fresh eggs when she was a little girl. It seems like a lot of faff for egg and soldiers. Thankfully there was bacon for their breakfasts, at least for the men, but this was via one of the family's pigs. My Grandad would make me howl in the seventies with eye-popping tales of how to sneak up on one and kill it correctly to make sure the meat didn't spoil. Childcare was a wild ride for Generation X kids. I would have preferred *Peppa Pig* on Nickelodeon, if that had been on offer.

I think of my ancestors' taste buds often as I prance through my ridiculous restaurant-critic life, bombarding myself with flavour from the moment I wake up. My cupboards are filled with titbits I've picked up while passing through Fortnum & Mason. I find it physically impossible to pass through that Piccadilly Circus food hall without splurging on their gorgeously buttery Chocolossus biscuits. There's something in the olde-worlde branding and spotting the liberal sprinkling of the 'By Royal Appointment HRH' symbol on the packaging that makes giving Fortnum & Mason your money feel like an act of self-love. For my daily groceries, I live breathtakingly close to a football-pitch-sized Asda with a 'world food' section offering snacks from Ghana to Gdańsk to Guatemala.

My great-grandmother didn't have a fraction of this choice. She lived and died before brands and processed snacks – foods designed to cuddle and comfort – took over the world. She didn't know the happiness of eating butterscotch Angel Delight straight from the sachet, with its synthetic smells and its delightful puckers. Nor did my great-grandfather know the joy of monosodium glutamate, guar gum, fructose syrup or the yummy-sounding E133 triarylmethane dye. And neither of them knew the term 'Greggs Yum Yum', and they certainly didn't taste a Starbucks Pistachio Crème Frappuccino, meet a Bombay Bad Boy Pot Noodle or ride a Doritos Cool Original wave. Nowadays, I can experience all of this of this by 10 a.m. at South Mimms service station.

The only trick my ancestors had up their sleeves to make food truly interesting was butter. When I think of Gran's house in the seventies, I think of boiled potatoes served with butter: just spuds scraped of their skins, never mashed, chipped or roasted, just boiled in a pan and served with butter. I think of thick slices of 'tea bread' made with sultanas steeped overnight in Lipton loose leaf, slathered in butter to help it slide down. I think of the two Jacob's cream crackers my Gran made for Grandad before bed each evening, smeared with what we could definitely describe as 'tooth butter'. They ate plain foods, served without flourish, but made delicious because of the butter, as it had been done for centuries.

As John Taylor, the Water Poet, wrote in *Epigrammes* in 1651:

> Great men large hopeful promises may utter;
> But words did never Fish or Parsnips butter.

This is an early version of the fantastically British put-down 'fine words butter no parsnips'. Parsnips are perhaps the greatest example of why butter is, beyond doubt, the original comfort food. There is a reason why the French see parsnips largely as glorified donkey feed, because an unbuttered one is an abomination. It is a skinnier, less alluring turnip. But load butter into the pan, let it melt and hiss, rattle some parsnips about in it and then let them crisp up in a red-hot oven . . . well, then alchemy happens. Then you have Sunday lunch and a nap in front of the fire.

I cannot say for certain whether my ancestors were more or less content with life than I am for having never tasted butterscotch Angel Delight pudding, but I know their life must have been much more straightforward. They lived without cars, dealing with the Cumberland weather and with scarce winter daylight, getting on with feeding animals, handwashing clothes and living for the tiniest crumbs of local gossip. It must have been tough going at times, but then each night at about six o'clock it would be suppertime. Everyone would gather around a big farmhouse table, which on good days would be laden with honks of fresh bread, plenty of butter, a slice of ham and some boiled and buttered potatoes: 'honest' food, as chefs always say when they've cooked something delicious with three ingredients (as opposed to the 'dishonest' stuff we eat every day in 2023). When I eat a homemade slice of buttery pound cake spread with more butter and damson jam, it's in my genetic make-up to love those homespun, straightforward flavours.

'But it was always off! The butter was rancid! It stank!'

As I paint this rather ambrosial picture of 'the good ol' days' of British eating, I can hear my now-deceased Mam's voice in my ear shouting the same thing she always did when she reminisced about 'the old folk'. This is what Mam, born in 1936, called the dour set of Victorians she spent every Sunday visiting for a church service and a high tea. 'Visiting' meant putting on a smart skirt and trekking with her mother, via bus, to Kirkoswald,

Lazonby, Renwick or somewhere else ten or twenty miles from Carlisle, to what she called 'the back of beyond'. She'd sit with one of her old aunts, or friends of her old aunts, women called Kitty or Biddy or Edna with stout bodies, big arms and walking sticks; they were well-upholstered women in smock dresses who had put on a brooch for their Sunday best.

The food on these visits clearly had its flaws. 'None of them had fridges!' she'd say. 'They kept their butter in a pantry. Everything was sour and curdled!' Butter stored somewhere too warm, too light or too damp quickly turns, but then no one liked waste so it wasn't binned. My old Great-Aunt Beatrice was the worst offender, apparently. Beat lived on cups of tea with floating lumps of mildewed milk and plates of suspect buttered toast, the pong of which entered the room before her.

At one old aunt's home – her name has been lost in the mists of time – my Mam was often given the 'treat' of bread and butter with a bowl of raspberry jelly made from packet crystals, which must have been terribly modern at the time. It was about 1942 and Second World War rationing was rife, which possibly explains this very tragic version of raspberry trifle. Mam said that the butter slathered across this bread was always past the turn, sitting in pools on her tongue refusing to go down, but she would battle on with the bowl regardless, as kids of the pre-Boomer generation learned to be seen and not heard. Their mere existence was annoying and the 'pensey' ones were the worst of all. Pensey, meaning 'fussy', was a word my mother's family used for any child refusing to eat something, however revolting it may have been: bacon rind, knobbly kidney, greying egg white, you name it. I can clearly remember Gran spitting the word 'pensey' at me with a curled lip in the eighties as I refused the disgusting salad cream she'd cobbled together from pickled onions and milk. There was definitely a shade of the Calvinist in my grandmother, a shade of the 'we'll rue the day for this!' Her saving grace was that she always had a good cake tin on the go, but ungratefulness and self-agency from a child were unthinkable all the same. My Mam ate what she was given.

All love stories have a beginning. My love of butter has a genesis that lives on in my mind to this day. If I close my eyes, I'm there in my multicoloured poncho and school skirt with black rubber galoshes on my feet. It's 1978 in Currock, Carlisle, and it's playtime for Year 1 at Bishop Goodwin Infant School. It's a dry day for once, and all the girls are on the playing fields, holding hands and spinning around. Jackie Swan, Karen Tait and I stop to grab handfuls of the buttercups that grow in patches from where the grass begins after the hopscotch courts, spreading like pools of honey. We take these buttercups, my little friends and I, and thrust them under each other's chins to find out if we like butter. The science of this feels a little hokey, even to a crowd of five-year-old girls, but as our chubby chins light up – some golden, some not as much – we squeak with happiness. We weren't prepared for it, but later that year we'd end up doing something far more exciting.

Good infant schoolteachers live in a crook of your brain for ever, albeit somewhat inaccurately. All grown-ups look ancient to tiny tots, and for a long time I remembered Miss Fullerton as a middle-aged lady with salt-and-pepper hair not long for retirement. She was in fact a lithe, enthusiastic twenty-two-year-old from Wales, fresh out of teacher training school and brimming with enough arts and crafts to make a Wednesday afternoon in Carlisle whizz by. She taught us how to make cute, plump Easter spring chicks from those squashy yellow Goldenlay polystyrene egg cartons, and she taught us how to borrow puddles of frogspawn from a local pond, raising them in jam jars before taking them back when the tadpoles sprouted legs.

Better than all this, however, was the day she taught us how to make butter. I'm sure when Miss Fullerton did this she didn't imagine that the small girl in the poncho, the one with the wonky home-cut fringe and the nigh-omnipresent stye in her left eye, might one day turn out to be a restaurant critic for the *Guardian*. I'm also sure she didn't think that the same girl would think of her butter lesson every time she sat in a Michelin-starred restaurant watching bespoke organic cultured butter be delivered to her on a shiny pebble. And I'm certain she can't have known that for the next forty-five years the girl would casually announce whenever the subject permitted, 'Oh, I can make butter, it's easy. You just need cream, a jar and the patience to shake it.'

The cream we used came from Bishop Goodwin's daily designated delivery of school milk. We arrived each day to find large red crates filled with dinky glass bottles sitting in the school's foyer. This was the last dying embers of the government generously supplying schoolkids with their third of a pint per day, which to anyone younger than me probably sounds highly peculiar. The mantra was that it was to keep our bones strong, although with hindsight it must also have supplied some of my friends with a decent chunk of their daily calories as poverty in Currock was, and still is, rife.

I loved school milk because I didn't like breakfast, so by 10 a.m., after a few rounds of Ring o' Roses and a session watching *Words and Pictures* on the big school telly, a tiny bottle of room-temperature milk went down a treat. It was cosy. At the top of these milk bottles was a layer of cream. It was the epitome of deliciousness to vamoosh this into your mouth with one short suck up a slightly soggy paper straw. Divine.

One by one Miss Fullerton had us all bring our bottles to the front and carefully pour our cream into a small Mason jar. It was as if we were concocting some type of witch's brew, and when the jar was about half full the hocus-pocus could begin. She closed the lid tightly, placed one hand in the air and began to shake the jar up and down with great exuberance. We all let out howls of delight. The woman had obviously gone mad, but the shaking went on, so she clearly was deadly serious.

We all stared saucer-eyed when she stopped and opened the lid after two minutes or so. We all peered inside.

'What can you see?' she asked.

'The cream is thicker!' we yelped.

'Yes,' she said. 'More shaking!'

For the next ten minutes the shaking went on, and she even allowed some of us to have a turn. I can still feel the nervous excitement as we all stood in the 'wet area' by the big white Twyford sinks with the stained overflow, the smell of papier mâché and disinfectant in the air. Lumps began to form inside the jar. The sploshing and knocking of the cream against the top and bottom had caused a delicious cream concussion. It sounded more watery inside. The buttermilk was dividing out, she told us. Yet more shaking, until she finally opened the lid once more to unveil something remarkable: a solid golden lump had taken shape.

We had actual butter! We crowded around with open mouths as Miss Fullerton drained off the buttermilk – to make scones at home later, she let us know – before plopping the lump into a bowl and rinsing it in water. She formed it into a circular lump with her hands. 'Shall we taste it?' she asked, knowing full well what our answer would be. She carefully spread the butter onto pieces of bread from a bag of white Mother's Pride and handed it round. We sniffed it dubiously, and then we ate. It was divine. God bless these incredible teachers who come into your world and create knowledge that lasts an entire lifetime.

Unlike my pig-keeping and crust-wrangling ancestors, I grew up with a local Co-op for groceries, a place that housed things like butter, cheese and yoghurt, complicated things that now happened far away in a factory somewhere. But despite that, we did not have butter at home. We had this other stuff which was yellow and soft. I returned home that evening to make an impassioned plea, but the answer was no. Mam said butter was inconvenient, that it was making us fat. Things were going to be different from now on. The Dents ditched eating real butter. My Mam became a Flora woman.

We were powerless in the face of Flora, really. It was going to make us thin! All the women in my family err towards enormous bottoms and those arms that keep shaking long after the last rah-rah-rah of the Hokey Cokey, and now we had the answer.

We were very susceptible to Flora's advertising as the telly was never off in our house. Telly was the background noise for the first eighteen years of my life. I'm sure that more genteel children's homes hummed with the delicate sounds of Vivaldi or a drama on Radio 4, but my house heard the Flora ad at least twenty times a day between *Crossroads*, *Celebrity Squares* and *Corrie*. The seventies slogan still lives in my brain today: 'Flora: The Margarine for Men'.

For a while the ads revolved around men nagging their wives to buy a tub as they'd heard it was so ruddy delicious. God forbid a man wandered into a shop of his own volition and exchanged funds for some. There was a strange infantilisation of dads in advertising throughout my childhood. Any man depicted putting powder into a washing machine or supplying a child with breakfast would soon be amid madcap chaos. Better to just let the ladies take the strain instead. There was, by turn, a weird truth in this. Dads were not in charge of buying groceries. In fact, I don't remember seeing a single dad in a supermarket until the late eighties. That's when the big supermarkets with hi-fi sections started appearing, and suddenly dads were lured in from their special chairs. Up until then, though, Mam chose everything, and she was very taken with Flora, its elegant white plastic container, airtight lid and the cheery sunflower on the side as if it was some sort of spreadable sunshine.

This was quite a big leap of faith, considering it was made in a factory by mixing chemicals with seed oils. Flora was high in polyunsaturates, low in saturates and low in cholesterol, not like nasty butter. Cholesterol was a big buzzword down our street back then. 'He's had his cholesterol checked . . . and it's up!' you'd hear someone's mother saying, talking about some poor dad who only recently had been cheerfully enjoying a Mr Kipling Cherry Bakewell in front of *The Chinese Detective* and minding his own lot. Now he was in a headband training for the Cumbrian Run and scraping Flora Light onto his toast.

Flora Light and all those other diet spreads were for people who found normal margarine wantonly indulgent. My mother and I were always on a bid to lose weight and so we downscaled further to Weight Watchers Table Margarine, which has a flavour I shall describe as 'slippery sadness'.

From around 1977 to 1989 the only British citizens making any meaningful defence of butter were a jovial group called the 'Country Life Buttermen' who appeared on ad breaks singing:

> Oh we are the lads from Country Life,
> you'll never put a better bit of butter on your knife,
> if you haven't any in, have a word with your wife!
> And spread it on your toast in the morning.

I rather loved this fruity, lumpen bunch of animated butter blokes popping up between *Name That Tune* and *Fresh Fields*, even if their song was about adding another chore to a woman's to-do list while they larked about with a squeezebox. I still remember how exciting it was at Christmas in 1984 when the Buttermen took over a whole ad break with an extended butter-based medley. Viewers even met one of their wives – who was inexplicably a sixteenth-century tavern wench – and the husband sang, 'She knows what I like, this wife of mine,' in a highly suggestive way. The Buttermen really tried to lead a national revolt against margarine, but with little success. As my friend Tim Worthington from the brilliant podcast *Looks Unfamiliar* always points out: 'They were made of butter, and they wanted everyone to eat butter. They were cannibals.'

The Buttermen's close-harmony singing made no impact on my household. The absolute opposite of a comfort eating memory is coming home in 1992 after a long day spent trying to decipher the political significance of Isabelle of Castille's peripatetic government for A-level history, then sitting in bed listening to *Little Earthquakes* by Tori Amos while eating two dark rye Ryvitas spread thinly with that Weight Watchers marge and half a can of lentil soup. Not even the full can! This was during a bid to get into a size eight Kookaï frock, and it wasn't worth it at all. The crackly, dry stuff coated with that insipid, yellow, pus-textured goo forced its way down my throat, but my stomach remained round. It was never flat like the women's on the adverts.

At around this time an advert for a low-calorie breakfast cereal used to shout: 'Can you pinch more than an inch?' The question reverberated in my head every time I stood sideways in the mirror, holding the extra parts of my hips. If I could go back in time now I would walk upstairs, shake teenage Grace Dent by the shoulders for five minutes and shout:

'You are seventeen years old with an hourglass figure and will never be this beautiful again, you fucking berk!' Then I'd make us both a round of thickly cut Asda tiger bloomer bread with centimetres of salted Country Life on top.

Yes, Country Life, not St Ivel Gold, which Mam moved on to after Flora. The ads for it showed us a sophisticated, pseudo-middle-class family with white smiles and visible deltoids running on deserted beaches in places that looked like Cornwall. We were not middle class: our house was pebble dashed, we all had silver fillings and we were more likely to be in Blackpool. St Ivel Lite – the diet version – tasted like static played in the back of a dairy parlour, but it was marginally more edible than Vitalite. Vitalite came in a big circular tub and, no matter how much you ate, it never seemed to end. Its advert was a spin on 'Israelites' by Desmond Dekker, except instead of the lyrics being about slavery and divorce they were replaced with promises of 'sunflower oil that will make youuuu shine'.

The most curious turn in this tale is when supermarkets began selling margarine with playful names like 'You'd Butter Believe It!' and 'Could It Be Butter?' These were – and still are – margarines marketed to women like my Mam who by this point can't really remember why delicious butter was shunned in the first place. They sit by the real butter in the supermarket for almost the same price and claim that, should you taste them, you will be frankly bewildered by their similarity to the real thing. This is, to use a technical term, bollocks. Aliens from the Planet Zaarg fresh off their spaceships could spot the difference between Aldi's Beautifully Buttery and a pack of Isigny Sainte-Mère unpasteurised salted butter, made with cream from cows who graze on the lush grass of Normandy's mineral-rich salt marshes. And nowadays we're told butter is healthy anyway: have you heard of its calcium-rich bone-building compounds? And the benefits of nutrients such as butyrate and conjugated linoleic acid? And how, if anything, butter is *reducing* the risk of obesity? Because if I eat more butter and less carbohydrate, then I can lose weight more easily by feeling fuller than if I ate large amounts of refined carbs. It's decided, then: it is daft to feel guilty about loving butter, because in moderation, it's really rather good for me.

And I know this at some level. I really do. It's just been a long, long road to get there.

———

Cooking and baking without butter is, of course, completely doable. I have made vegan cakes in the past, incidentally, with moderate success. (My vegan croissants, however, we won't be discussing.) And Queen Nigella in *How to Be a Domestic Goddess* whips up a heart-stoppingly good courgette cake with little more than three grated courgettes, olive oil and bicarb. The cake isn't green, it's gloriously moist and you don't miss the butter at all. Don't ask me how she manages this: like everything La Lawson does, it is just mesmerising witchcraft.

And so, in good faith, having lambasted margarine for much of this chapter, I will now introduce one solitary caveat for when it is better to use it. There is only one known example: School Dinner Puddings.

On the podcast my guests return time and again to the subject of school dinners. Jay Blades was particularly fabulous on his memories of the dining-hall serving hatch at his Islington comp, the sights and the sounds of hot chips being scraped from stainless-steel pans, the sausages and pies loaded onto plates still warm from the dishwasher. School dinners are important. They're a social occasion and a break in the tedium, stressful as hell for some and the one moment of bliss in a day of drudgery for others. Jay's true joy when he thinks of this time was reserved for the school-dinner puddings, and margarine *always* had a role to play in them.

And I'm with him on that. I can picture the rudimentary jam sponge cut into lumps and served with custard drawn from a large jug with a ladle, or the vivid yellow of a Tottenham cake with its bright pink iced topping strewn with cheap desiccated coconut. I pine for the mint-green custard we'd pour over the sumptuous traybake that would be offered on any given day. In my book

Hungry I wrote about the volatility of comp schools in the eight-ies: the bullying, the fighting and the distinct lack of hope and ambition for a brighter future. But all that would momentarily disappear when, in the middle of the day, a bell rang and we'd all eat crude flapjacks made with margarine, oversized porridge oats, golden syrup and sultanas – or, better still, Bakewell tart flapjacks with yet more marge, a scattering of almonds and a thick carpet of blackcurrant jam along the perennially underbaked shortcrust bottom. These tastes will live on in my brain fondly and for ever.

My personal heaven in the eighties was the classic Carlisle school traybake 'Australian Crunch'. You needed to be sitting on table one or two in the dining hall to get a slice – any later and supplies were wiped out. Australian Crunch was, again, mostly marge, but this time combined with cheap cornflakes, coconut, syrup and a thick layer of atrocious-quality chocolate topping that set in ridges across the top. We were never told what this stuff had to do with Australia – someone told me it was invented in Bolton – but Australia seemed pretty glam for those of us in the North watching a lot of *Neighbours* and *Home and Away*.

Right at the tippy-top tier of my school-dinner comfort eating life, though, was 'Chocolate Concrete', a slapdash, laugh-ably rough-and-ready take on a chocolate brownie, complete with crunchy edges, a chewy centre and a blanket of granulated sugar pressed into the top – the sugar was pressed on by hand by a woman called Donna wearing a flip-top sovereign ring from Elizabeth Duke at Argos. Chocolate Concrete should *never* be made with butter. You need margarine oil that comes in a four-litre bottle with a name like Whurl, or with a label that says 'Baking Marge – 12.5 kg: Code 40653'. You can make chocolate concrete with butter, and it'll still be delicious, but it will taste a bit like it's tried to dress up nicely for a court appearance.

The best Chocolate Concrete is made by taking 200 grams flour (not self-raising, and not 00 fine; do not sieve it, just hurl it into a bowl), adding the same amount of granulated sugar (not caster sugar, never demerara; who do you think you are, Princess Charlene of Monaco?), followed by fifty grams of cheap drinking chocolate (no, not Green & Black's, for God's sake). Mix these dry things together, then pour in a hundred grams of melted margarine and stir. Don't even bother with an egg. Posh recipes sometimes ask for one, but just don't bother, it's a waste. Bake it in a lined pan for approximately fifteen minutes at 160 degrees, preferably while talking to a woman called Doris about why Sheila's thyroid is playing up again. Whip it out when it stops looking like wet mix and leave to stand for fifteen minutes. *Zut alors!* as the *Tricolore* textbook said: you're done.

Butter simply won't deliver the same experience. It won't give you 'goths trying to look aloof while carrying a tray of sausage, mash and spaghetti hoops', and it won't give you 'everyone banging their plates and yelling as some kid has dropped a tray and then someone else has skidded in a pool of bean juice'. When I make it with marge I get blasts of my second year at Caldew School, feeling very hot and bothered over a pop star called Michael Hutchence who I saw in *Smash Hits* wearing cycling shorts and baring his chest beneath a leather jacket. Chocolate Concrete is hair crimpers, Body Shop kiwi fruit lip balm, swapping *Sweet Valley High* books with your friends and begging your Mam for a new batwing top from Clockhouse at C&A to wear to the school disco, where you'll likely end up dancing to 'White Wedding' by Billy Idol.

(Sidenote: I have also tried to recreate the pink strawberry custard accompaniment to Chocolate Concrete with Madagascan vanilla pods, strawberry Yoplait and squirts of Dr Oetker pink food colouring. Eventually I was tipped off that eighties school dinnerladies used cheap pink blancmange powder, adding water to make it runny. That's it. That's the taste. That's the colour. Sometimes with comfort eating, making things badly is making them *exactly* how they're supposed to taste, and margarine is an exact taste from a specific point in time.)

While Jay did speak blissfully of the marge-loaded school-dinner syrup sponges, the snack he brought for the show was bun and cheese, which to the uninitiated is like a large, thick, sweet hot cross bun. He demanded it to be spread thickly with real butter. Here was another person, I felt, who'd been on a journey with margarine, but now treasures the taste of real butter.

For much of my life, then, I lived like I was taking part in a dress rehearsal, stoked by self-denial, self-sabotage and procrastination. The turning point in my butter journey came via a crowd of Puritans and a talking goat. No, really.

I love lying on my sofa in the dark watching horror movies, even if this love changes shape to terror the following morning when, as a writer, I'm left home alone behind my laptop. Loved ones leave for work and all of a sudden I'm in a silent house jumping at every bump in the attic.

This is the price you pay for watching films like *The Witch* (2015), starring Anya Taylor-Joy. It's one of my absolute favourites and I urge you to watch it – you will never look at butter the same way again. *The Witch* is about a clan of religious zealots in seventeenth-century New England. They're part of the tub-thumping bunch who fled England after 1620, seemingly in search of less comfortable lives with stricter rules and a worse diet. Not all religious enthusiasts are like this – I've spent my life around Anglicans and Methodists, and boy do those people love a potted meat sandwich and a slice of rhubarb pie – but for these God-fearing folk life is self-induced misery. For most of *The Witch*, they're next to starving. Several failed harvests offer up nothing to eat but groundnuts, acorns and anaemic asparagus, and all their rabid praying is rewarded with spindly vegetables and terrible wheat, which make pallid stews, watery soup and dry bread. Their diet, their life, is the height of tedium. And then the devil shows up in the form of a goat called Black Phillip with an offer up his sleeve. He's got something better than angels and scripture.

'Wouldst thou like the taste . . . of butter?' he asks the eldest daughter. 'Wouldst thou like to live . . . deliciously?'

The word 'butter' drips with lusciousness, with decadence. God forgive me, it's just plain sexy. Runny, sating, pleasurable. The golden nectar that lifts the spirits and transforms the gloom on this failing farmstead in the arse-end of nowhere, washing over your taste buds and making your heart thump.

It's everything they are against. Comfort and joy, cosiness and happiness, putting oneself first. Butter seeps into every knobble and crevice of their meagre meals, making the tough, the fibrous, the cruciferous and the frankly underripe taste like a treat rather than a chore.

Butter, richness, unbridled sweetness and the wanton thrill of taste buds erupting. Butter is quite literally taking the cream at the top of the churn for your own selfish ends . . . and why would anyone do this? Who do you think you are!? Butter is the brazen temerity of enjoying the act of eating instead of grimly subsisting, while keeping your mind on what Saint Peter might say at the celestial gates.

I won't spoil *The Witch* for you, but when Black Phillip showed up with his offer those Puritans didn't stand a chance. And as a person who went without the good stuff for significant periods of time, the devil's offer truly spoke to me.

Because I want to live deliciously too.

The best bit of fancy dinners – although I never write this – is often the bread at the start and the butter that goes with it.

Posh restaurants can be a little stressful. They require a lot of smiling at aerated goose skin, clarified gel and lamb tendon, as well as a lot of genuflecting at the chef's genius – and then you pay a £300 bill. I hope I don't sound too ungrateful saying this. Complaining about being a restaurant critic always sounds like Scarlett O'Hara in *Gone with the Wind* whining about her dress ribbon not being floofy enough.

But the best bit really is that polished pebble I mentioned earlier. The pebble that appears after you've waded through all the hassle of finding a bra, getting dressed, leaving the house, paying the congestion charge, getting stuck in the Dartford Tunnel, arriving, parking and making pleasantries with all the front-of-house people, before finally sitting at a table with your dinning companion feeling rather hungry and ready to eat. And then, then, it appears: the pebble.

'So, before we get going,' the server says, 'this is our home-made malted sourdough, baked fresh. It has a smattering of semi-candied sesame seeds across the top, and the bottom is crisp as it's pan-baked in vintage loaf tins that the chef's nan saved when fleeing Alsace in 1936. And, to go with it, some fresh cultured honey butter, churned this morning using cream from the nearby dairy that we collect by hand from a farmer who keeps rare Belted Galloway cattle. The honey is from our own beehives. Our queen bee is called Matilda. Enjoy!'

And then they just leave you. You're alone with two large slices of thick, moist, dark bread that looks a little like chocolate cake, and about 200 grams of the honey butter, as if to say: 'You don't strictly need to eat this now . . . or at all. It is an accompaniment to your fancy dinner. And you certainly don't have to eat *all* the butter. Because that is a lot of butter. You can't eat it all, surely . . .'

They leave you sitting there listening to the soundtrack from the French film *The Intouchables* played by Ludovico Einaudi on piano, looking onto a view of the restaurant's organic kitchen gardens. Oh gosh, it's all very affable. And then before you know it you and your dining companion have eaten all the bread, along with the entirety of the butter, the whole honking lump, devouring every gram, pushing the remnants of it off the knife and into your mouth with your fingers before pushing the pebble back to the server sheepishly. A lot of posh restaurants will try to take you on a journey of tastes, scents and textures that will be new, challenging, sometimes exciting and occasionally just downright unpleasant. I firmly believe that the 'butter on fresh bread' course is the only thing that keeps diners calm and feeling secure. I'll wager that not one person who ate the live ants crawling over the plates at three-Michelin-starred Noma in Copenhagen enjoyed them, but it was the bread and butter course that stopped them from rioting.

All the above happens before the actual courses begin to appear, which of course contain mountains more butter. That's why, even when a fine dining place is all weird and overwhelming, you still get a flickering feeling that you're in your kitchen at home on Christmas Day treating yourself to the last smear of the very good buttery pâté or spreading rum butter on panettone in your jim-jams with *Morecambe and Wise* on in the background. That's why restaurant food is so very good: they add *much* more butter than anyone would in their own home. You didn't see the golden lake of butter in which they basted the scallops, or what they loaded into the *pommes aligot* or the hollandaise, or what went into that sticky toffee pudding's unctuous life-enhancing puddle. The same is true with the pasta with sage butter and salted ricotta at Benoli in Norwich, and the slow-cooked leg of lamb in anchovy butter from Morito in Hackney, and the rich, vibrant pistachio butter-grilled baby gem at Milk Beach in Soho. Yes, you can even smear lettuce in butter, and it is bloody lovely.

I made sure Mam got real butter every day when she was getting on. We had stopped bothering with Weight Watchers after her first cancer diagnosis in the mid-noughties. It was hard for Mam to get het up about being 'beach body ready' after the Cumberland Infirmary had taken one of her breasts, and medical students by her bed in white coats were pulling faces that suggested starting any long novels like *Riders* by Jilly Cooper would be ambitious. She proved them wrong and lasted another fifteen years.

In her final days, in 2021, I smeared butter on Warburtons toasty loaf and slices of Cumberland plum bread, and we would lie in a double bed together eating the good stuff while we watched re-runs of *A Place in the Sun*, the show where people from Dunstable dream of a life in Alicante, and so they go to Alicante with a thin TV presenter to look at three depressing villas with no natural daylight before deciding to stay in Dunstable. This was my mother's absolute favourite show.

'I'd knock that back wall down,' she'd say as I measured out the morphine, 'and put a breakfast bar in.'

We both put on a lot of weight. Me from sugar and white wine, her from steroids. Learning that you can get fatter on your death bed was a life-changing thing for me. I always saw dramatic weight loss as the only upside of my eventual passing. The last six weeks where I looked like Grace Kelly would make the grim final push worth it, I thought, but it turns out this isn't a given. It made those long months of smearing Benecol Light on Slimcea loaf in the nineties feel extra futile. There was no margarine in those last days.

A year later, Michael Ball, one of her favourite celebrities, appeared on *Comfort Eating*'s Christmas special bringing a snack of panettone with very, very thick butter. An annoying thing about losing someone you really loved talking to is that you never stop having fresh news to tell them, and no one would have enjoyed news of Michael's visit more than Mam. He painted a picture, with his snack, of one of the very happiest things in life: taking his dogs out for a walk and a wee on the morning of Christmas Day before coming home to slices of thick, clove-scented fried bread, laughing away in the kitchen with his family.

'There is something in the enzymes that makes you lose weight,' he laughed, clutching his belly.

After he left, I smeared the leftover panettone with tooth butter and thought about my Mam as I devoured it. I relish life's highs when I can these days. This isn't a dress rehearsal. So when the pebble comes at the restaurant, I eat it all, down to the last smear.

Russell T. Davies's

Butterpepperrice

Comfort Eating could very well have its own special spin-off show about writers and their grottily satisfying deadline snacks. Writers are experts at staring desperately at a blank Word document and willing it to fill up, pining for comfort food that delivers self-love and sustenance. There's not a hope in hell of them putting a julienne attachment on a Magimix, or even putting on actual pants and vising an Asda.

When I was holed up in a regional Holiday Inn Express during the last stages of writing *Hungry* I ate little more than watery instant porridge – Quaker Oat So Simple cups to be precise – with random handfuls of sultanas and packets of Splenda hurled in. Boiling a kettle and filling the paper cup to the defined line was all I could cope with while trying to finish a book that reflected upon both Findus Crispy Pancakes and Alzheimer's disease. I ate this precisely every two hours, as if I was at a Victorian workhouse subsisting on a fancier genre of gruel.

Russell T. Davies knows about tricky deadlines all too well. His writing schedule and prolific output make me feel like an underperformer. He wrote *Queer as Folk* in the late nineties, smashing down boundaries of how gay men were represented in TV drama, before going on to write *Doctor Who* and *Torchwood*. There's also *Years and Years*, which to my mind is one of the finest TV dramas written this century, while Davies's recent drama *It's a Sin*, about a group of British friends in the eighties living through the AIDS epidemic, moved audiences at a seismic level. There was something about the deathbed scenes of the character Colin that was so real, so well observed, that I couldn't quite bear to watch them in a newly bereaved state. The staring, the surreal outbursts, the hopelessness. It was too much. Davies is a master scriptwriter.

His writing snack, when he came on the podcast, was a three-ingredient dinner made from items you'd find in even the most desolate of kitchen cupboards. 'It's butterpepperrice,' Russell told me on the very first episode of *Comfort Eating* in his glorious Swansea accent. It's exactly what it sounds like: butter, pepper and rice. No other ingredients are necessary, and yet somehow it sounds like a feast rather than a list of ingredients. We talked about him making this 'recipe' for his boyfriend Andrew when they began spending more time together behind closed doors. And how Andrew laughed when he first found out about this comfort food. We both agreed there is a stage in every relationship in the beginning when you have to reveal what you really eat. And it is *so* exposing.

Russell cared for Andrew in his final days following a brain tumour diagnosis, and we spoke about how love changes shape during this caring process. How it's no longer nice days out and parties and household admin that take life forwards, but instead a tight routine of feeding and pills and naps. We talked about how it is hell and tragic and draining, yet at the same time beautiful and useful. It is filled to the brim with love. And then suddenly it's over, which is momentarily a relief given that your loved one is no longer suffering, but then immediately you miss it all: you miss the waking up tired, already late for the morning's pill dispersal, and you miss the surreal chats and the plates of thickly buttered toast in bed, and you miss the daily routine of waving that person goodbye in incremental steps. You miss them. You just miss them.

THE RECIPE

200 grams white rice
Butter (no specific amount here, just go with God)
Black pepper

Cook up white rice (it can't be brown rice, it simply must be white). If feeling lazy, use an incredibly handy packet of pre-cooked white rice; if feeling extra fancy, use Tilda basmati rice.

Admire your rice, lying there all plush and fluffy. Isn't it satisfying?

Now add butter. Let's say Welsh butter in honour of Russell himself. Salted. If you really want a measurement from me, I'd say add a wodge, or a medium-sized kerchonk. An amount that makes you want to begin eating the rice immediately off the back of a wooden spoon despite the fact you've not left the kitchen yet. Just make sure to be generous with it, aka put in as much as you want.

Admire the now honey-coloured rice. Poke your nose in and envelop yourself in sweet, fragrant scent.

Add pepper. I'll be fussy here and say no pre-ground black pepper, as it will overpower the butter and make everything the colour of silt. If you have a pepper grinder, then hooray. Preferably it is one of those oversized grinders that you bought from Lakeland because you thought it would be sophisticated to have it on your countertop like Rose Gray at the River Cafe probably did, except now every time you need to put more peppercorns in the piddly little hole you end up festooning the entire kitchen with them, and then the dog farts them out for days afterwards.

Mix everything and pop it in a bowl. Eat while rereading today's writing output, sighing loudly over the fact that a team of marmosets tied to several laptops could come up with more satisfying pacing and structure than this pish you've created.

Feel comforted by the butterpepperrice; allow it to soothe you.

Close laptop and fall asleep with full belly, without brushing teeth as it feels too much like admin.

Try again tomorrow.

PASTA

. . . And Why It Serves as an Act of Self-Love

Noodle Doodle came to town with lots of straight spaghetti
Twisted it around and 'round
And this is what you getti.
Noodle doodle doodle doodle . . . motor cars!
Noodle doodle doodle doodle . . . houses!
Noodle doodle doodle doodle . . . butterflies!
Eeeeek!
Noodle doodle mouses!

Pasta is the most unreliable narrator of one's true appetite. It was designed by the gods to trick you into eating slightly more than you really need. Or maybe it was the devil playing a trick, making a hundred grams of dried pasta look like little more than a meagre handful. Those pasta-measuring implements where you poke spaghetti through a hole certainly feel like a good idea as you're parting with money for them, but when it's just you and that measurer alone in a kitchen at dinnertime, it suddenly feels like it's judging you.

It really is impossible to overstate how lovely a cheap bag of penne can be. That penne that has soaked up the very best of the mush which you've concocted after a hard day from just a tin of tomatoes and a handful of dried herbs well past their best – they were practically potpourri, but somehow it all worked. There it is in the pan, beckoning you back for another forkful as you pass by while taking your plate to the sink. You tell yourself you should put the leftover portion into Tupperware for the next day, but try as you might, you just can't do the right thing. You know it won't taste a fraction as good tomorrow. This is your moment.

And so, out of nowhere, in a delicious flurry of carbs, you find that you've consumed far more than the 'recommended serving amount' (whatever that means), standing right there at the hob. You sheepishly glance at the clock. This isn't an internationally recognised mealtime. It's 11.06 p.m. But afterwards, don't you sleep so much better? Doesn't the duvet fit just that little bit snugger? Aren't you content?

Obviously, eating pasta close to midnight is frowned upon by dietitians, Italians and women called Tamara in neon headbands who do 'power yoga' and want you to have 'killer abs'. In fact, eating anything at all after 8 p.m. is unfashionable these days when you could be 'opening your fasting window', which to me sounds like a hot new buzz phrase for an idea as old as time itself: being hungry. I have gone to bed hungry many times in my life longing for a tiny, perky bottom, lying fitfully under the covers and dreaming of the next morning when I get to measure out forty grams of Grape Nuts with skimmed milk. Needless to say, I've had enough of that now. I have tried the 18:6, the 16:8 and every other fasting ratio under the sun. Each time I have failed in this diet and fallen backwards into bed replete with my brother David's pasta bake with sausagemeat bolognaise, eaten straight from the Pyrex dish while loading up the dishwasher. David is a brilliant, instinctive cook, although he never follows a recipe or makes anything the same way twice. For me, that's proper cooking. His sauce has everything thrown at it bar the sink's Brillo pad: ketchup, honey, stock cubes, Dairylea and so on and so forth, until it melds to make an unctuous, rich brown sauce that wraps around giant conchiglie like edible velvet. It's enough to make a volatile wildebeest lie down for a nap. Or a hungry big sister. Nothing beats a post-pasta soporific fug.

Recently I've even heard an expert say that pasta, as a source of nutrition, has so little that is favourable about it that it should be viewed more as a leisure activity than a food. She said that creating a large feast of pasta for your friends offers the same spiritual sustenance as inviting them all over to watch YouTube clips of dogs surfing: you might all feel happier, but none of you had even a soupçon of vitamin K or dietary fibre in the process. The experience, in fact, was void.

This type of subversive talk has no place on the *Comfort Eating* podcast. If pasta is a pursuit of leisure then my listeners are avid hobbyists, and some of them could even take it semi-professional. My body cries out for pasta like it's carb-loading for the Marathon des Sables, which is unfortunate seeing as I spend much of my 'working life' propped up in bed behind a laptop surrounded by snoring cats. Most days I'm one down from 'sedentary' on the activity level categories.

The problem with pasta is that it doesn't have any problems. It's perfect. It's readily available anywhere and everywhere, be it garage forecourts, tiny minimarts or even that newsagent on the corner that only seems to sell lottery tickets. Each of these places probably has some form of budget pasta sitting on a dusty shelf. Is it out of date? Who cares. Pasta will outlive you. If they found a bag of pasta underneath one of the pyramids, it would probably be OK if you boiled it for twelve minutes and grated some Parmesan over it.

It's also a design classic, a bland but intoxicating conduit for creamy, tomatoey, meaty, cheesy things; if you hurl sugar, cinnamon, nuts and dried fruit at it, you've got a sweet Kugel pudding; if you throw nothing at all aside from a drizzle of olive oil and a skoosh of salt and pepper, it might look drab but it will still be thoroughly decent. Pasta is so utterly easy to cook it can be done on autopilot, or with a hangover, or while crying, or shortly before giving birth, or with one hand swatting away the previous things you have given birth to. Pasta can be cooked by teenagers, when they're at that level of syrupy zombie brain growth where the only things they remember are who they fancy and where their phone is. And when these teens hit their twenties, they'll notice that a big pan of pasta will feed an entire crowd, at Eurovision viewing parties or World Cup viewing sessions or basically any occasion where one has announced, 'Yeah, let's all do it at mine, I'll cook!'

As my parents began to age and lose the impetus to cook, I always knew a microwave ready meal of chicken arrabbiata or spaghetti carbonara was the safest of bets to put in their fridge: it was filling, delicious and a good source of carbs and calories, and if the label said something like 'Finest' or 'Marks & Spencer Gastropub' then they felt it was an absolute treat. When Saoirse-Monica Jackson from *Derry Girls* came on *Comfort Eating*, I loved that she made us the very dinner she used to make for the rest of the show's cast, in her flat, after a long day of filming: a pan of spaghetti, feta and Tabasco, which on the face of it doesn't sound much, but was irresistible. Long after Saoirse had gone home and my producers had packed the mics up and left, I served the leftovers as dinner to my other half, Charlie.

'This is incredible,' he said, licking the last drops of sauce off a spoon in the kitchen. Why do I bother with fancy recipes, I thought. Pasta, something saucy and a load of cheese: always does the job.

In the past, pasta has been my chief technique for self-soothing. Back in the nineties, when I was in my mid-twenties and worked in women's mags, we didn't talk very much about mental health in the workplace, aside from when we'd shout helpful things at each other like 'Get a grip', or gossip that one of us was a 'loony' or some other such slur. In my first years living and working in London it is safe to say I teetered on the edge of depression a great deal of the time. I was rabidly ambitious, yes, but so was everyone else I met. I was skint, unconnected, but worked with precisely thirty-seven young women called Arabella Blinkinton-Wotnot with fathers who ran Time Warner and aunties who designed alpaca-hair hand-bags. My contemporaries wore vintage Dior and Michiko Koshino daywear, and I wore bootcut trousers in flammable fabrics – whatever was on sale on Oxford Street. I had credit card debt, totted up in order simply to exist and pay rent for a flat above a building merchant in Bounds Green, which was so unfashionable and so far from Kensington that my col-leagues struggled to believe it existed. Aged twenty-seven, the only thing I cared about was finding someone who wanted to kiss me, more than once, and getting my name in a byline in a fancy magazine. Instead, I spent much of the late nine-ties single and earning money by opening the mailbag at *Chat* magazine, where readers earned £100 for real-life stories about their botched tattoos.

If it's a comfort eating dinner for one you're after, on a day of such twenty-something angst, I do wonder if there is such a thing as a bad plate of pasta puttanesca. Puttanesca is the gloriously frank Italian name for the pasta sauce that one makes by sloshing half a tin of tomatoes into a pan and chucking in various salty things – capers, anchovies and the like – as well as some chilli powder for good measure. It translates as pasta 'in the style of a whore', apparently. I can't imagine knocking off after a day's work in a Sicilian bordello and searching the streets for a jar of capers, but that's just me.

To my mind, though, this is a recipe open to change. Puttanesca is what I call any one-woman-sating ad hoc pasta sauce. I could make this with a love bite from one of the boys at *Loaded* magazine while waiting for him to call me on a landline. (Spoiler: he didn't.) This particular iteration of the sauce would contain a softened onion and maybe even a red pepper, along with a few olives and those budget-price big pasta tubes – rigatoni – which you're supposed to boil for eight minutes and serve *al dente*. Back then it was likely I'd be distracted by Martine McCutcheon screaming on *EastEnders*, though, so the pasta would be *al dente* only to the toothless. Still, what the hell, it tastes wonderful, especially when eaten while on the sofa. Inevitably, the sweet, vivid red sauce would find its way down my pyjama top. This can sometimes lead to finding remnants under a breast when one eventually showers, though perhaps it's only me who finds boob rigatoni.

Later on, in the noughties, when I hit my thirties and began working as a newspaper columnist, my pieces would run with a photo of me looking furious with big hair at the top of the page, and I started to get invites to be on telly. It was only natural that my tastes started to become a *little* more fancy, and so I developed a decadent spin on 'whore's spaghetti' which I call 'butterslut' pasta.

This is the kind of dinner you throw together at 9 p.m. when you realise you haven't done all the things you were meant to have done by the time you hit your thirties, when you really thought life would be simpler but instead you're unmarried and have no time to have a baby because your work hours are getting longer, and on top of that you're hearing reports that your father is forgetting things and leaving front doors open. It's the dish you need to have up your sleeve when you remember that you haven't kept in touch with your school and uni friends. It's for that moment you realise you're meant to be a diligent auntie and godparent while also spending every weekend at another wedding, lavish hen do or baby shower while scrabbling money together for a deposit on a tiny studio flat, which you have no time to view and will never afford as you've wasted every spare penny on mismatched fucking ramekins off Cindy and Tom's fucking John Lewis wedding list. Oh, *and* you've noticed that your boobs aren't as perky as they used to be.

Your thirties are stressful. Have you thought about eating some pasta?

Admittedly I thought twice about sharing this recipe's name with you, as I'm unsure whether butterslut, in modern parlance, is problematic, but finally being cancelled from public life over a pasta sauce name seems like an opportunity for true notoriety and headlines. With that being said, I could achieve the same thing by strangling Jay Rayner, and believe me, his jazz piano version of 'Ol' Man River' has driven me towards it . . .

Before I reveal all, I should say that butterslut pasta possibly breaks some of the Golden Rules of Comfort Eating because I do mine in my pressure cooker. I like to put it on when I come in from *MasterChef* and leave it to do its thing.

What I'll usually do is finely dice a shallot and soften it in some butter (you can use white onion if no one's looking – I'm not sure if you can tell the difference, I just know a shallot is more middle class). When the shallot is translucent I add some tinned tomatoes; if you can, use the Polpa ones as they're delicious, but KTC or even Asda Smart Price tinned tomatoes are fine. Then I add some more butter. A lot of it. More than I would like to admit.* I do all this softening and stirring on the 'sauté' setting of the pressure cooker, then I add drained olives, put the top on, set it to twenty-five minutes and let it steam cook.

Yes, my slut's pasta contains a full jar or tin of black, pitted olives. Pitted, incidentally, means the ones *without* the stones. This is terribly confusing if you are an olive novice. I know 'unpitted' sounds more logical, and 'destoned' would be a better word, but I didn't make up the silly rules, nor the fact that we're still following them in the 2020s. This sounds like the fault of someone like restaurant critic William Sitwell. Yes, let's blame William. The reason I need to pressure cook these olives is because this is a last-minute *Comfort Eating*-style recipe that uses the ones in jars from the dustiest shelves of the aforementioned minimarts – the ones that left Greece sometime before the millennium and were bottled in an Albanian factory before spending some years in a cargo container at Zeebrugge. But I

---

* For my reasoning surrounding the butter, please return to the chapter entitled 'Butter' and read it again. And this time make notes in the margin.

am not a snob about olives. Yes, I love those fancy pea-green, perfectly shiny, fancy Nocellara ones, but to me any olive is a miracle explosion of umami. I did not eat an olive until I was at least twenty years old as we didn't see them much in Carlisle. I do remember the Dents once adventurously adding some to our build-your-own Asda pizza – it put the rest of my family off them for ever more, and even now my brother David distrusts them completely and calls them 'shit grapes'.

Anyway. Once that's all done, I add handfuls of fresh egg pasta, a godsend in any fridge as it takes just two minutes to cook. And there you have it: each forkful of butterslut pasta is restorative, just as any roughly assembled pasta dish after a long, cold day is a bold act of self-love.

Eagle-eyed gourmands may have spotted that not one of the pasta dishes mentioned up to this point has been authentically Italian. For this I can only apologise. My generation did this, not my Gran's or my Mam's. They may have dabbled with pasta, but it was Generation X who embraced and vandalised it. In a pre-internet world I thank God the Italians were not fully aware of the horrors we were up to with their beloved cuisine, or else the entire population of Genoa might have marched upon Carlisle.

They'd have found me stirring jars of Dolmio 'white sauce' into pasta shells, not realising that this was béchamel, the thing that is supposed to go between the meat sauce and sheets in a lasagne. I'm so sorry, Naples. Or they'd have caught me pepping up penne with a judicious dollop of smoked salmon Philadel-phia. When I search for 'Italians mad at food' on the internet

I wince at the proud people of Sorrento, Milan and Palermo shouting abuse at Brits serving linguine with ketchup; for many years, I swore that throwing baked beans in spag bol was perfectly OK, and deep down I secretly still do.

In truth I can never be snooty about Dolmio, or Homepride or Loyd Grossman sauces for that matter, because when they first began appearing on shop shelves in the North they gave families like mine a penchant for adventure we previously didn't have. Northerners love moist food, and now pasta had its own gravy! *Now* we understood it. At around the same time our local Fine Fare began selling loose pasta in huge bins, allowing you to serve yourself different shapes. The bins were marked with names like 'shells', 'curly' and 'cowboy hats'. Northerners were not to be trusted with the Italian names. We'd just get ideas above our station.

Mam instantly brought home a sack of the brown wholewheat penne that her latest Rosemary Conley fitness plan said would get us thinner. This tasted like damp cardboard so we only ate it once before it was relegated to living at the back of the cupboard for the best part of a decade, sitting alongside last Shrove Tuesday's Jif lemon and a jar of Camp Chicory & Coffee Essence.

When I think of pasta dinners in the earlier stages of my life, I think of my first proper tastes of culinary creativity and self-agency. I am thirteen years old, lying horizontal on the sofa by myself watching *Brookside* and *Whose Line Is It Anyway?* while my parents work late, eating a bowl of pasta in 'sliced mushroom ragù', a bright red sugary sauce advertised by opera-singing Brits at a dinner party; the rain drums against the windows and the small lamps in the living room make it very cosy as I leaf through a copy of *Just Seventeen*. I'd finish this whole sophisticated feast off with a Müller Fruit Corner. Bliss. And so grown up. Soon enough I was experimenting with a chopped red pepper, some sliced courgette, a handful of grated red Leicester or a Knorr stock cube to pop in with my fusilli and make it taste herby. None of this was remotely Italian. But was what I made comforting? Yes. Definitely.

In the noughties, I made my first tentative steps into proper food writing and I discovered some home truths about pasta. Pasta could be an elegant thing. Chefs like Anna Del Conte and Rose Gray came into my life via fancy cookbooks, whispering that food from Puglia or Florence was not about just hurling around Cheddar. It should be delicate; it required cogitation; it needed deft seasoning and a fine *soffritto* base. They told me I should stop putting baked beans in pasta and instead serve white beans, simmered for hours with bay leaf and rosemary. Other books suggested that the local Carlisle *ristorantes* that I loved, with their salmon fillet fried in sambuca and their dough balls with garlic butter, were not 'proper Italian'; they said garlic bread was definitely common, whereas bread soup or ribollita was humble peasant food and ergo brilliant. In London my expense account took me to grand Italian restaurants like Locanda Locatelli in Marylebone where the *linguine all'astice* cost £40 for a few strands of pasta, and although that dish was heavenly I couldn't help but miss my home town's Casa Romana where the carbonara – made with streaky bacon and UHT cream – came in a healthy portion for £5 a bowl, and you could wash it down with warm frizzante.

In truth, I'll never stop finding British-Italian food truly comforting. Brits know in their hearts that Antonio Carluccio was right, that pasta sauce takes time and love. We suspect that good pasta sauce requires the patience to shave garlic cloves with a fine razor like a jailed Brooklyn mobster with time to spare, like we saw in *Goodfellas*. But we also love 'Italian food' with rudimentary red sauce, whether poured out of jars or eaten at places with wipeable menus and red tablecloths. We want overcooked pasta with a side of deep-fried breaded garlic mushrooms, and we want someone with an Italian accent to grind an enormous pepper mill over our spag bol, knowing full well that they are not a fraction as Italian-sounding when they're talking in the kitchen.

I've eaten pasta inelegantly all my life. Yes, *sometimes* I do wish I was one of those food writers who spent their childhood in Tuscany learning about Italian gastronomy via a cherished housekeeper or earwigging on their parents' glamorous dinners. Those people always instantly hold more gravitas when they speak about food, but then there's nothing about life in late twentieth century North-West England that isn't faintly hilarious in print, and I would not swap a single, solitary second.

Holidays were not gastronomical adventures when I was small. If we were lucky we might get as far as a chalet at Pontins holiday camp in Southport where the canteen served lumpy mash and battered 'fish slice' fourteen times per week, after which there'd be a 'Dance with Your Dad' competition. Or sometimes we'd go to a small hotel in Rhyl, North Wales, where I'd eat a sugar dummy on rope during a day trip to Llandudno Pier. Or I'd have a Wall's Cornetto at Liverpool International Garden Festival, and then it'd back to Kirkby to see my Scouse Nan, who'd have brought out the Rover Biscuit Assortment.

At the pinnacle of all this was Silloth on Solway, a seaside port town only twenty miles from our front door in Carlisle. Silloth holds a special place in the heart of millions of Northerners and folk from south-west Scotland. For me, it's the Las Vegas of Cumbria. We'd leave the urban landscape of Currock, Carlisle, with its graffiti and pebbledash, and very quickly we would end up somewhere filled with shops that sold buckets and spades and ice pops. There was a penny arcade with one of those push machines where you might win a ten-pack of Regal Blue King-size with a fiver Sellotaped to it if you fed it enough twopence coins, and it always felt like 'holiday time' because the shops sold naughty postcards of women with large boobs having their bottoms felt. And that's without mentioning the chunky little van – not remotely like a normal ice cream van – which roamed the streets selling homemade ice cream from a company called Longcakes, giving us a chance to have raspberry ripple in a little cone. Sometimes we'd go to the tea rooms and Mam would buy us a jam tart and a glass of banana Nesquik, or we'd eat fish and chips wrapped in the newspaper sitting on the bonnet of Mam's British Leyland Princess overlooking the Irish Sea.

In the summer, whenever the sun shone, we'd be down to the beach on the firth, building sandcastles on the dunes close to Sellafield until our skin peeled. Then, when the holidays finished, we'd return to school, only to be taken back there on our official school trip! Yes, back to one of the only places we'd ever been, but this time to look at the port and carrying tracing paper to do rubbings of stones.

None of this, though, compares to the excitement of Easter 1979, when the Dents spent a full fourteen days in Silloth. Mam took me and my little brother for an extended sojourn in a static caravan. I thought it terribly brave of her to take us on her own, although I look back now and understand she was simply sick to the back teeth of my father with his asthma and his moaning and the never-ending washing pile; she'd found one snotty hanky shoved down the side of the settee too many, I fear, or seen too many a mardy face from Dad when Liverpool FC had been beaten, and fleeing to Silloth was less hassle than a divorce.

It was an ambitious April trip and the forecast said that it would be raining the entire time. Terrific winds would be blasting across the Irish Sea, liable to knock our caravan on the Stanwix Caravan Park off its stand or us off our feet each time we ventured to the shop. Mam, however, was determined. We weren't bothered by the rain at all, because the thing about caravans – and the reason why I still love them today – is that the more it rains outside, the snugger you are inside. Rain just made it even more exciting when Mam would fold out the caravan table to serve our lunches. It would invariably be something out of a tin, and it was almost always pasta on white toast. A lot of the time it would be ravioli: small, plump envelopes of salty, mole-coloured stodge; or Noodle Doodles that came in the shape of butterflies and houses, which we'd eat while singing the advert; or just classic spaghetti hoops. You cannot beat spaghetti hoops in that 'tomato sauce' which tastes nothing like the original fruit. That delicious blend of modified cornflour, citric acid, sugar and garlic salt is a flavour that is imprinted in millions of British hearts and minds.

Tinned pasta is always on my online grocery delivery and it's available in every supermarket when I am far from home. It is my saviour when I am sad and tired, when hotel room service has stopped serving, when I can traipse to a Tesco Metro and back with those small tins of Peppa Pig spaghetti that I can eat with a hotel teaspoon. Whoever invented the Peppa Pig spaghetti shapes needs to be knighted. They need their day at Buckingham Palace. They created a tinned pasta experience where the sauce clings to the little chunky pigs much closer than it does to hoops, making the whole dining experience stodgier and more satisfying. They elevated the culinary experience of so many everyday humans, and their ingenuity needs to be honoured.

Tinned ravioli has a particularly special place in my life. It's basically adult baby food, inauthentic as pasta to the point of being a different beast altogether. I still don't know what's inside those delightfully slimy pouches. I don't want to think. It's not twelve-hour beef daube, that's a definite, but the soft, sweet mushiness of it slipping down my gullet, lining my stomach, is filled with memories.

Tinned ravioli is day nine in a static caravan. The rain has poured to such an extent that the parking area has flooded. It is very exciting. We are adventurers. We don't even notice that Dad isn't here (not that he can call us to check in, what with the nearest phone being the pay booth beside the shop). Mam buys us fishing nets on sticks and tells us to go to the puddle and find dinner, which keeps us distracted for hours, and on other days we just play Top Trumps in bed.

Tinned ravioli is my Mam making tea and reading us *James and the Giant Peach*, or Pam Ayres's poems to make us laugh: 'Oh, I wish I'd looked after me teeth,' she'd say, doing Pam's West Country accent. It's Kid Jensen on the radio and us dancing to 'Physical' by Olivia Newton-John, or watching *Starsky & Hutch* on a portable telly. It is the smell of fusty, dusty caravan cupboards and being cosy under covers. It is the Friday night and Dad rocking up, sheepish, getting a lift to the camp site off his mate Terrence. He appears at the window with a plastic bag on his head as a makeshift waterproof, soaked to the skin. Mam spots him and bursts out laughing, and then they're both laughing, and they appear to have missed each other. She calls him a 'silly sod' and he calls her 'mein Führer' and 'she-who-must-be-obeyed' (the classics, of course), and then he tries to kiss her loudly, which makes us kids squeal with horror. She goes 'GERROF ME YOU SCOUSE GIT,' and everything is lovely again.

I sit on Dad's knee as he reads me today's Andy Capp comic strip in the *Daily Mirror* and Mam makes us all ravioli on toast again. Tomorrow, she says, we'll go and get ice cream in Mary-port. Mam says we can have a packet of Guinness World Record stickers to try to complete our albums. I need a Number 1 sticker, the world's tallest man, to complete the first page. Mam says they probably haven't printed any Number 1s to make her buy more packets of stickers, but that can't be true. I can't imagine a world where grown-ups would be so mean. I eat the pasta, scraping the sauce off the plate with the most marge-smothered piece of the bread. It is wonderful.

Silloth is a constant as the years pass. I am taken as a tween, less impressed by the penny arcade and the little van with the raspberry ripple, and then as a sullen teenage goth in the eighties, only there as I can't be trusted not to have a house party if left alone. I walk along the beach, twenty metres behind Mam and my father, fuming that I am not in Berlin hanging out with the Sisters of Mercy. In the late eighties my parents splash out to buy their very own static caravan and spend every weekend on the beach, walking their dogs, listening to Foster and Allen

CDs and eating microwaved spaghetti hoops on Warburtons with Utterly Butterly. And then I'm there, back from university, finding Silloth bizarre, trapped in time, heroically quaint but also a little depressing. In the noughties they have to get rid of the caravan as Dad can't go any more – he has dementia and it's too much for him, and with Mam and her health it's a bit too cold. Still, sometimes we drive out there for chips and a walk. We go very slowly down the seafront, holding Dad's hand so he doesn't get lost and suggesting to Mam that she use a wheelchair – she won't be seen dead in one, she says, someone might see her and think she can't walk any more!

And then, after microwaved pots of spaghetti hoops eaten on toast one Saturday morning for breakfast, I load into the car with my two brothers, all of us older, greyer, heading to Silloth. We park the car where their caravan once was, hop out and make our way on to the sand dunes, walking over the wet sand and staring out far into the Irish Sea. It is a blustery February day, the rain coming down, and there's no one else here. We throw Mam and Dad's ashes into the wind, watching them disappear in seconds.

Life is impermanent, and everything changes. I love tinned pasta because I like to cling to the small things that are constant.

Gaz Coombes's

Tuna Pasta Bake

Interviewing rock stars is nerve-wracking. It's part of their job spec to be sexy, alluring and charming – if they didn't have that special something, then no one would stick them at the front of the stage and use them as something for the rest of the band to hide behind. As an interviewer you're supposed to be immune and aloof to these things, but I had Gaz Coombes from Supergrass stuck to my fridge at uni, pouting in tight trousers, with his cheekbones distracting me each time I went to rustle up a bowl of Crunchy Nut. Ah, Gaz Coombes, the cat-eyed rock god, the crown prince of glam rock-tinged jangle-pop; dreamboat, troubadour, front man – now, twenty-five years later, he was coming to my house.

Frankly, I was now much past my best looks-wise, and certainly not in a position to marry him, or go to the Good Mixer pub in Camden together, as I had imagined us doing in the nineties, high-fiving members of Blur and Suede and appearing on the front of *Vogue* as a Britpop couple to rival Liam Gallagher and Patsy Kensit. And yet, all the same, I was nervous as hell about having Gaz round. Rock stars evoke the law of the schoolyard in us: you can't help but want the cool kid to like you. I quickly realised this wasn't the place to do a hard-hitting Emily Maitlis-type interview, but what I could do was welcome him into my living room, make him a cuppa, and get him to tell me some stories about food.

Gaz transpired to be funny, warm and forthcoming about life on the road with Supergrass – and yes, he was still sexy, but I hardly noticed this as I am a consummate professional. I was starving after a morning of frantic cleaning, so Gaz's special tuna pasta bake was very welcome indeed. A word of warning, though: if you are hoping to look coquettishly alluring, I cannot in good faith recommend eating a bowl of extra-large conchiglioni pasta shells baked in a creamy sauce of Campbell's condensed cream of mushroom soup and mozzarella. Yes, it is completely delicious, but the oodles of melted cheese will form strings from the plate to your mouth, and that's without mentioning the Walkers ready salted crisps topping that will flake off in lumps and set on your décolletage as you try to ask sensible questions.

I loved Gaz's choice as it had a classic hallmark of what makes a perfect *Comfort Eating* food: this 'TPB' is a hark back to his mother and her family dinners. Between the ages of five and eight, Gaz and his family lived in San Francisco, and his mum picked up that very American style of cooking that calls for adding tins of mushroom or chicken soup to recipes to make a 'cream' sauce. It's a technique that is still wildly popular in the United States, and even some of the fancier recipe books will gloss over onerous preparations of béchamel sauce or chicken stock and just tell you to hurl in a full tin of the good stuff. The result is a decadently creamy dish, hitting all the notes of 'getting home after a cold walk from school' and 'being off sick and getting lunch on a tray'; in this specific case of deliciousness, it clings around the pasta shells beautifully and settles in puddles within them, so that every mouthful makes you return for more.

Gaz makes this recipe for his wife and daughters all these years later, especially when it's grey outside and everyone needs cheering up. Rather wonderfully, Gaz's family live in the same house his parents owned; there's a sense of history repeating itself as he goes through the motions of getting dinner down on the table. It's a ritual, he says: he boils the pasta, opens the tin of mushroom soup, chucks in the mozzarella and, of course, adds the tuna, which breaks down to become almost invisible while giving the whole thing a rich, fishy, umami taste.

THE RECIPE

(serves four hungry people)

800 grams conchiglioni pasta

1 large onion, diced

75 grams salted butter

2 × 160 grams tins tuna, drained

1 tin Campbell's condensed cream of mushroom soup,
    diluted with 400 millilitres milk

250 grams mozzarella cheese

1 packet Walkers ready salted crisps, roughly crushed

Black pepper

Begin preheating oven to 180°C/fan 160°C/gas mark 4. Feel like a grown-up. Realise you have no idea how the oven warns you it is at the correct temperature as you tend to shove everything in before it's actually preheated. You are *not* doing this for this recipe. That's called growth. Well done you.

Boil the pasta. Read the packet to check how long and then do it for slightly less, as it's being baked in an oven and you want it to keep some shape and firmness to be able to make those lovely rockpools of fishy sauce. Set the pasta aside.

Melt the butter in a saucepan, add the onion and fry gently until the onion goes soft, pale and a little translucent; if you have patience, it might even go a little golden. Go easy on the heat and don't burn anything as it will ruin the gentle, comforting flavours of the dish – easy does it . . .

Plop in the can of soup. It will lie there in a quivering lump, as though it were a dismayed jellyfish. Mash it down a little and add the milk. Increase the heat and begin to stir until it becomes a sauce. Add a little water if the sauce is feeling very thick.

Add the tuna and carry on stirring. Throw in half the mozzarella and carry on stirring. Pop in the black pepper, and quite a lot of it – Gaz's version had a real kick.

Add the pasta. Stir the whole thing up into a terrific, delicious tuna pasta train wreck.

Tip this hot mess into a greased ovenproof dish. Add a sumptuous roof of crisps, and then add the rest of the mozzarella to the top.

Bake for 15–20 minutes until the cheese on top is golden and starting to brown.

Eat on a cold day, in a bowl, with a spoon, shovelling it into your mouth like a starved wildebeest that has been migrating across crocodile-filled swamps for weeks and has only just reached the lush, grassy savannahs of Kenya.

Eat a second helping.

Eat the rest of the pasta while allegedly making it into a packed lunch for tomorrow.

Sleep like a baby.

BREAD

... The Comfort Food Celebrities Apparently Don't Eat (But Really They Do)

Of all the foods that celebs bring to my house, the bready ones fit the 'secret snacks' brief most closely. *Comfort Eating*, I say right at the start of every show, is about the things we eat when nobody's looking, and believe me when I say that celebs *do not* eat bread when anyone is looking. I have sat in many a fancy establishment dutifully doing my job as a restaurant critic and watched as the breadbasket is foolishly offered to people who wear tight clothes for a living. You may as well offer them a tank of live piranhas.

Consuming lovely, filling, carb-loaded bread has become deeply unfashionable and is increasingly viewed as being borderline reckless. Yes, it may have been the cornerstone of planet Earth's daily diet for thousands of years, and perhaps it is one of the cheapest forms of sustenance we have access to and therefore a vital tenet of the Lord's Prayer, but this doesn't mean Kylie Jenner or Emily Ratajkowski would ever eat a big chunk of Asda tiger loaf; the supermodel Gisele Bündchen has probably never eaten a Warburtons giant crumpet with passionfruit jam, and that's her loss.

I do accept that some people have actual medical issues with bread, and they have my full sympathies. Those who make the voluntary choice to not eat bread, however, cannot be trusted. These people give off the message that they're a special superhuman type of person putting in a bid to be flawless. They're running their body like a sleek racing-car engine, ready to pose on a glossy mag cover or make a guest appearance with Elton John at Glastonbury at any moment. The rapper Drake will no doubt have them on his yacht in Barbados this summer – that is, unless they make the cut for *Love Island* and spend summer held captive in a villa with a lot of other people who don't eat bread, being asked, 'What's your type, mate?' by Zack from Cleethorpes. Zack doesn't eat toast, but he does eat a kilo of grilled chicken per day.

Personally, I run my body less like a sleek racing car and more like a 1973 Austin Allegro: vintage, classic and still able to get me from A to B with a little warm-up. It's for these reasons that I still choose bread every time, and it was also for these reasons that I was ecstatic to welcome Self Esteem into my house for a cheese and onion sandwich on white bread with a dipping ramekin of salad cream. Likewise, I cheered when Jo Brand, one of my favourite famous people, arrived with her snack: 'the fried bread sandwich'. Oh, hallelujah! Bread on bread on bread! I shall unveil the recipe for this later on in this chapter, as it is a thing of wonder.

And for anyone who still thinks eating bread isn't sexy, well, I challenge you to watch Hollywood star Rafe Spall concoct and then devour a Cathedral City and Branston sandwich on Co-op wholemeal and not find it even a little bit erotic. We spoke about fame, denial and body image; about how we want our stars to represent 'normal people' on screen, but at the same time, we want them to be far thinner than 'normal people', i.e. humans who are on calorie-restrictive diets almost all the time. For that short moment in time, though, sitting around my kitchen table, Rafe ate like nobody was watching, washing everything down with a dirty martini. He looked so incredibly happy. Probably because eating bread is just utterly blissful.

I will admit that I have led, many times, a bread-free existence. Let me be the first to tell you that bread-free days seem to last longer and feel darker, and eating becomes less happy and more complex. Because although I love the accompaniments – the runny baked beans, the strawberry jam, the oozing Brie, the buttery scrambled eggs – the fact is that without the bread itself there is nothing for these things to rest on. Baked beans just look damn peculiar on a plate on their own; it is the buttered toast that transforms them. Scrambled eggs need a plinth to raise them up from eggy goo – which is actually quite unpleasant if you focus on it – to a fabulous treat of a breakfast. Bread is not just something to use to make a plate look fuller: it is the secret star of the show.

When I give up bread, I give up some perfect comfort eating moments, like my lunchtime trips to the cheap and cheerful Roti King next to Euston Station where they serve Malaysian roti canai: bowls of fragrant dal with flaky, fresh piles of roti. *That* bread, in conjunction with *that* dal. Oh lord, have mercy. There are queues round the block every day from 11.30 a.m., and no one is queueing just for the lentils. I also lose the slices of sweet, fragrant Irish soda bread in my brother's kitchen, smothered in extra-strong Cheddar spread and dotted with sweet chilli sauce. I lose those lovely lunchtimes with friends pushing a Pizza Express Fiorentina pizza into my mouth, the drippy egg mixing with the wilted spinach. I lose my mother-in-law's amazing fluffy sunset-yellow homemade challah bread with honey on Saturday mornings, served with gossip and plans. I lose Pret a Manger croissants with my morning coffee as I rush to a meeting, half starved, and I am no longer permitted my Pret 'posh Cheddar' baguette with its layer of mayo and pickle – yes, I know it's 651 calories, and I know it's so crunchy and difficult to fit into your mouth that it can cause grievous harm, but I will persist. Sometimes I want a sandwich to hurt me, dammit.

Above everything, though, when I forgo bread, I lose white toast. Every mundane day should have a pocket full of happiness, and I think white toast brings this by the bucket-load. It's a marker of how comforting and delicious white toast is that people sound so guilty when they choose it.

'White?' the waitress asks, writing it down on her pad in the cafe.

'White,' you'll say, with a micro-expression that really says: 'Please don't judge me. I know I should choose the thing that is browner, lumpier and less appetising. I know I should have the thing that is harder to chew. I eat brown bread all the time, I swear. My bowels are the dictionary definition of regular. Let me live, damn you!'

White toast, we have been told, is for the uncivilised and the foolhardy. It's for the sorts of people who don't know the meaning of 'multigrain', 'sprouted', 'dietary fibre' or 'Hay Festival'. White toast is what posh people might eat in the event of a war after enemy troops have pillaged their sourdough starter.

In the event of a conflict, I would rather head straight towards the Drawer of Deliciousness in my freezer cabinet and pull out that emergency loaf of Warburtons white that sits among everything else that does emotional heavy lifting for me when times are tough. Every home should have emergency white toasty bread in their freezer sitting ready for action. Nothing soaks up tomatoey bean juice like the buttery crusts of white toast. White toast is the bedrock, the impetus, the catalyst, the safe space on the plate when everything else is a little too much.

There is no situation that cannot be made more manageable by the smell of white bread, coming back to life, browning in the toaster, filling the kitchen with hope and thoughts of butter, raspberry jam, Marmite or Nutella. White toast is for those moments when you find yourself leaning against the kitchen cabinet and taking stock of your day, those moments when you think, 'This can't possibly be it, can it? There has to be more to life than dreaming up ways to avoid the office summer baseball party and paying off scraps of my credit card bill.' And then the smell of white toast drifts from the toaster, escorting you back from the brink.

I haven't even mentioned those breadsticks and slabs of moist focaccia that you get given in non-fancy Italian restaurants. Nor have I mentioned crumpets, soft and puckered with deep holes to fill with butter, nor the Scotch pancakes which send me back to Pontins holiday breakfasts watching *Why Don't You*.

Quite simply, without bread, I lose the swiftness and simplicity of being full. Without it, my life is all toppings and none of the bottomings. Without it, my life is full of the moist and the sticky but none of the crunch and chew. Life without bread feels unnatural.

When I am in a bread-free phrase, and when I am being the type of person who says loudly, 'Oh me, I don't eat bread,' I'll inevitably wander into a Sainsbury's one morning to buy cat food and toilet cleaner, and all of a sudden I'll be hit by the aroma of baking white rolls. Yes, I know it's merely pre-made dough loaded frozen from a truck, mass produced in a factory many miles away and shoved into an oven for twelve minutes on 200 degrees while 'the baker' is on aisle five doing a stocktake, but I do not care. Those fresh white rolls are heaven. The thought of this bread is more enticing, more delightful than anything that has passed my lips for weeks.

I load four of the rolls into a paper bag with the tongs. They are still warm. I walk back to the house picking at one with greed, telling myself that if I was French this would be the height of sophistication. And in my kitchen, I pile butter, slices of ripe Brie, a layer of mayo and some bright yellow piccalilli into the fresh rolls' crunchy shells, lifting them into my mouth one by one, swallowing in large bites like a enthusiastic baby hippo eating a watermelon. The spell is broken. I am a bread eater again.

And don't even start me off about what I'm like in a Greggs.

The smell of baking white flour goods communicates with me at a very fundamental level. All of those shops and cafes know exactly what they're doing. It's a non-specific smell of salty, sweet cosiness that speaks to a part of you that you've tucked away and forgotten.

Fresh white bread in particular, no matter how cheaply made, is my way back to being a kid again. I often get sent back to happy times with my grandmother, with her white curly hair and sharp tongue, though in reality not all times with my grandmother were happy given that she could be quite irascible, pithy and stubborn (like a lot of seventies grandmothers). She wasn't cuddly or twinkly at all, and she wasn't remotely catered for by the seventies birthday-card market, many of which would say: 'Happy Birthday Granny, your cheery smile lights my day. I know you love me in every way!' The elderly women I knew as a child were puff adders who had lived through a long world war, rationing and TB outbreaks; they were women who, if need be, could act as the local midwife or amateur undertaker. They'd seen a lot, and put up with a lot – and now they sat about in floral-print smock dresses, with their enormous arms and pernicious anaemia, being judgemental and finding new ways to be disappointed by their daughters, sons-in-law and grandchildren.

And yet, despite this, in Gran's favour is the fact that she was hilarious: unintentionally so, but funny nevertheless. And she loved – *loved* – drinking tea and eating sandwiches and cakes in cafes, so if you wanted to get around her, the chief tactic was to pick her up from her house and drive her somewhere with a view where pork tongue was served in a bap and iced white buns were available for afters. And if there wasn't a view of something pretty, like a lake, she would settle for a view of other human beings, whom she would instantly dislike. (Gran could hardly walk; she'd had a bad leg since she was a child, and very few people cared about mobility issues back then. There was a sort of unspoken notion that disabled folk should just stay in the house and not attempt ambitious things like shopping or going to the cinema.)

We often went to a bakery called Oliver's as there was parking close by and the tables had enough space for her to get behind. A cornucopia of baked goods awaited us as we went through the door: white loaves, bread baps, stottie cakes, French sticks, wholemeal loaves, farmhouse bread encrusted with seeds. The mood was hectic, and the staff – who wore bottle-green uniforms with flat Victorian caps as a nod towards *Oliver Twist* – were always working flat out, but by God it is the smell that I remember. That smell will always mean happiness to me, always mean jubilance, always mean let's treat ourselves, sit down, drink tea and gossip.

In Oliver's Gran could hold court with her brown varnished stick and her enormous white leather handbag. The handbag contained every piece of paperwork she'd ever come across, as well as the deeds to her house, her premium bonds and a family tree; it was basically her version of the internet.

I miss my Gran immensely. Her memory is sealed in my heart, even if I was never sure that she liked me.

'You've got a screw loose, you,' she'd say, perusing me over her Cheddar and piccalilli barn cake as I read my *Smash Hits* magazine.

'Don't say that to her!' my Mam would say.

'Well she has! She's not normal. With all this pop music and singing to pop. When I was her age, I was doing a bit of doily and making a coaster.'

My Gran's answer to almost all parenting issues was doing 'doily'. This was a long-winded Cumbrian pastime where you fed wool through a wooden bobbin with four pins in it, and after some sort of magic everything cohered into a place mat. Gran's attempts to get me doing doily were disappointing. I would tangle the wool, lose the end of it and get distracted by Duran Duran on telly.

'She's got two left hands, this one,' she'd say. 'She needs her head tested.'

'Don't say that to her!' my Mam would say again. 'You'll give her a complex.'

This was another big feature of a seventies or eighties childhood: being 'diagnosed' and threatened with being 'carted away to the big house' at least twice a week. It has taken me a long time, almost five decades in fact, to realise that none of us are normal. I am not remotely normal, and neither are you, quite possibly. The least normal person I knew as a child was my Gran, and this is why I loved her. I loved how she slipped you fifty pence when no one was looking and sang 'The Old Rugged Cross' in a mournful manner as she did housework. I loved her enormous beetle brooches and her ability to see a very old man across Oliver's eating a ham bap and say, 'See him, he wet his pants in school in 1921, we all had to move desks.' I loved how hard-line she was about other people having flippant, silly fun, without ever quite explaining the thing that had happened to her to make her such a cynical, vehement teetotal. I loved how she questioned the staff in Oliver's about their goods, constantly asking them: 'How long's this bread been sittin'?' And I loved when she ate pease pudding with slices of stottie cake and told me about the war, about how she would make tea for the prisoners of war being held at Hadrian's Camp while they were out doing 'chores', because even though she loathed the enemy, it turned out some of them were 'real nice folk'.

When I smell bread baking anywhere, it takes me here and back to her. To bumpy memories of an odd lady, an odd lady that I'd give anything to speak to now.

When the comedian Fern Brady came on *Comfort Eating* and talked about her life and her autism diagnosis, the snack she brought was simply a loaf of white Kingsmill, still in the plastic bag, untoasted and with no butter. She plucked slices from the bag and ate them, explaining that the soft, bland uniformity of each slice has made it something she's always loved to eat, especially when she feels overwhelmed. Fern's choice – so simple and straightforward – has made me see plain white bread in a whole new light, because I shall never forget her sitting in my living toom with her loaf, looking staggeringly beautiful, speaking in her gorgeous Bathgate brogue – a type of Scots that you rarely hear on telly or BBC Radio 4 – about the challenges of being neurodiverse in media.

'People call me and say, "Fern, is this a good time to talk?" and I feel confused because, well, yes, of course it is a time to speak. I have picked up the phone. I don't understand the question. Why would I pick up the phone if I could not talk?'

Fern usually opts for cheap white bread, the type of bread that's available in most places, be it a corner shop or a twenty-four-hour garage.

'I could have got you sourdough or something nice!' I said.

'No, this is the one – the cheap one is the best.'

And I think she's probably right. I have eaten those expensive, pillowy bloomer loaves, the ones that cost £9 from bakeries that are painted pink; those bakeries that use 'ancient grains' and make the staff wear Japanese workwear dungarees; those bakeries where they fling walnuts and pumpkin seeds at their bread, where the yeast was hatched from a 'mother' that has been carted around the Cotswolds by a woman in a Boden dress who has her own outdoor kiln; those bakeries that only open from 9 a.m. until 2 p.m. from Thursday to Saturday and make you feel grateful for being there.

Lidl white loaf is more comforting, I think: cheap white bread can sometimes be enough. Bread does not need to be flavoured with Guinness or sun-dried tomatoes, or plaited or puckered or encrusted with candied pecans. Cheap white bread is the opposite of difficult or worthy. It is the thing you reach for when you want a sour emotion or jagged edge cushioned.

It would be remiss of me to talk so much about bread and not discuss the humble sandwich in a little more detail. In my view, the greatest, most comforting sandwich is mushed-up boiled egg with salad cream on buttered white bread, cut into four squares. Not triangles, and not halved horizontally, no – the sandwich must be in four infantilising quarters. You possibly have your own opinions. Perhaps you prefer a wafer-thin ham and mustard, or raspberry jam with a layer of butter, or tuna with sweetcorn and almost too much mayo. But you'd be wrong.

Mushed egg sandwiches were what my Mam made me for packed lunch on the school trip to Lightwater Valley amusement park. It was one of those trips that the teachers held over your head for the whole term, saying they'd kick you off it for being naughty. The day of the trip came and we'd set off bright and early at 6 a.m., and by 6.25 a.m. on the M6 someone already had their Tupperware out, flooding the bus with that unholy egg-sandwich fart smell which hung in the air and got everyone accused of letting one rip. Oh, the shame, the humiliation, when you didn't even have proper Tupperware cos your mam didn't go to those fancy Tupperware parties. I'd been sent with my sandwiches in an old Asda ice-cream carton. Mam had tried to peel the label off but now it just said 'SDA NILLA', and Rhona Harrison noticed and then everyone laughed. (Rhona Harrison had a fancy box that popped and locked with a matching Thermos mug.) And yet even when contained in the old ice cream box, those mushed egg sandwiches were delicious: creamy and eggy and buttery and soft, cut into four squares and served with a packet of ready salted crisps. Lush.

Mushed egg sandwiches were also what my Mam made me during the long summer holidays, the ones that seemed to last for half a year. The kids on my street would have impromptu picnics up on the field we called 'the Lanky', and if I asked very nicely Mam would break off from ironing or sewing and make them for me to take and share. She'd carefully boil the eggs until they were rock hard before whacking them on the stainless-steel sink and shelling them; then would come the unmistakable sound of repeated thwacks on the bottom of a Crosse & Blackwell salad cream bottle. All the kids brought something: diluted Kia-Ora orange squash in an old SodaStream bottle, two Club biscuits, that sort of thing. Other kids had to be more inventive, bringing anything they could steal while fleeing the house: stale white bread in a bag was a classic, with no spread, no butter. We'd feed that to the local travellers' horses. Some mams were not keen on 'feeding the street', but my Mam turned a blind eye to that. She was fierce, yes, but she was generous. No stray cat or sad child stayed hungry for long.

Any time I see egg sandwiches now, I'm catapulted back to those days with no sun block, no phone and no radio contact with my parents from 10 a.m. until 5 p.m: days that felt endless, though they weren't without their troubles. I'd be out arranging cut-grass piles into the rooms of a princess's mansion with my friends, with one square shape serving as the princess's dressing room and another triangle shape as the ballroom. I can picture my Mam moving about the kitchen with a cardigan over her nightie at dawn, cobbling together Dad's 'bait' before work:

'Christ, George, this fridge is empty, when are you getting paid?'

'Thursday – can we get through to Thursday?'

'Jesus Christ, are we broke again?'

'I've got a fiver in my jeans pocket. Do we buy food or do we buy petrol?'

'Well, we need petrol or you can't get to work,' Mam replies. 'Hang on, I've found three eggs that aren't off. Well, at least I think they aren't off . . . what date it is now? Oh, that's this coming Saturday. I'll do you some sandwiches.'

And then she's off creating magic, pulling something out of nothing: two eggs mushed up on white bread for Dad, and the third mushed up in a cup with salad cream and white bread soldiers for me.

I once believed the Marks & Spencer's pre-packed cheese and celery sandwich to be the pinnacle of sophisticated human eating. It was all about the crunch and the bitterness of the celery and the way it paired with the soft white bread. As an eighties teen I would eat one each day on my break from selling Bic biros at W. H. Smith. They stocked very few of them, probably because nobody was as worldly as I was, I thought. When I grew up, I told myself, I would eat cheese and celery sandwiches all the time, and *never* mushed egg sandwiches. They were for babies.

Oh, eggy salad cream sandwich, how I rejected you. I came to fancy London in the nineties and the trendy continental sandwich bar was in full swing, offering me wobbly slices of buffalo mozzarella on ciabatta with fresh rocket and chicken breast with pesto on granary bread. I felt so chic with my sandwich from MacCray's Deli on Hatfields when I worked at *Marie Claire* magazine. This is *exactly* how they do it in New York, I thought; this is exactly how Amanda de Cadenet does it. I would join the lunchtime queue while playing Snake on my Nokia 8310, smirking at the chopped egg option behind the glass. What sort of loser would choose that when there was feta and olive on sourdough? When there was pastrami on pumpernickel? Why would I eat white bread with mushed egg now I was a cosmopolitan woman?!

But you were always waiting for me, little egg sandwich. You didn't take offence. I make you now when I get in from work. Never overfilled, just small and delicious and humble. Not pretentious, not wasteful, no notions of grandeur. A treat to be eaten while lying cocooned in a duvet, watching the telly.

I still eat the centres of the sandwich first and leave the outer crusts till later. If I don't eat them, I can hear Mam in my head telling me that my hair will never grow curly.

'I don't want curly hair!'

'Shut up and eat them,' she'd say. 'There's kids starving out there.'

Jo Brand's

Fried Bread Sandwich

Making the *Comfort Eating* podcast was always a slenderly veiled way to hang out with people I've rated for a long time, and reader, Jo Brand is one of those people. When I was a little girl, I used to watch the Channel 4 comedy show *Saturday Live*. It was presented by Ben Elton, and it was an anarchic comedy cabaret show with the likes of Rik Mayall, Ade Edmondson, Harry Enfield and Julian Clary performing, and occasionally they were joined by a woman dressed in black baggy clothes.

Jo Brand – or 'the Sea Monster', as she called herself on stage – was a neat summation of all the things that made some sections of Thatcher's Britain furious. She dressed defiantly 'unsexily' (so they said), donning bovver boots and political slogan T-shirts, and to make matters worse a lot of her routine was about how she really hated men. The sheer guts it must have taken for her to go out on the comedy circuit and ram this routine down the throats of drunken stag nights and bemused builders on the Friday-night lash boggles my mind.

In a way, seeing Jo was a real turning point for me, and for my comfort eating philosophy. She was one of the first examples of a woman not really caring if men liked her, and I realised that when you remove the constant pressure of being deemed fanciable by complete strangers, you free up your brain to think about more important things. This meant a lot to me as a young woman, even if I spent the following twenty years hoping to wake up one morning miraculously looking like Audrey Hepburn. As I age, I understand it more. Some women complain furiously about being invisible after forty, but I rather like no longer hoping for the appreciative nod of a gaggle of lads as I walk past. It's fair to say that I'm enjoying my 'Sea Monster' years.

And now, all these years on, Jo was coming to my house to share food with me. I had met her before, once, when we were on *Have I Got News for You*, although that show is so stressful I can remember little about it beyond standing at the side of the stage with her and Paul Merton thinking: 'Why do I agree to these things?'

Jo appeared having driven herself directly from a friend's father's funeral, carrying a loaf of white bread, butter and a bottle of brown sauce. We talked about everything from mothers, teenage rebellion and awful boyfriends to mental health and the time she burned her flat down – but what really struck me was the snack she brought with her. Why do we not eat more fried bread sandwiches? Civilisation has missed a trick!

My father adored fried bread and always pestered me to make him some, which I did while telling him that it was terribly bad for his arteries and his cholesterol, half-heartedly offering a bowl of All-Bran Bran Buds and skimmed milk instead. Obviously, I'd give my eye teeth to make him a plate of fried bread and tinned 'sketty' now.

THE RECIPE

The following recipe is what Jo and her friend used to make in their bedsit while ludicrously hungover. I have written it in tribute to that.

(makes one sandwich)

Three pieces of plain white bread – preferably the spongy stuff that is still forty-five pence a loaf, with a slight sheen when you hold it to the light as it is made of wheat mixed with emulsifiers like mono- and diacetyl-tartaric acid diglycerides and flour treatment agents.

Butter. As much as you like. Lots.

A bottle of brown sauce. Perhaps HP, perhaps Daddy's brown sauce, perhaps some other type of generic sauce – as long as it is tart, fruity and full of vinegar, molasses and tamarind. (NB brown sauce isn't strictly meant to be enjoyable. It is a sort of endurance test and deeply symbolic of the British psyche: check us out, adding brown abrasive sludge to our food to make it slightly difficult but ultimately more character-building to eat.)

Open eyes. Take in hungover aftermath of big night out. Be quietly proud that you not only took your shoes off and clothes off but also did not cause any incident involving the fire brigade, à la Jo Brand.

Realise that you are somehow simultaneously starving, dehydrated and in need of a wee. Recall that you kissed someone last night who you could not pick out in a police line-up. Experience remorse.

Go to kitchen. Open and close fridge door many times in hopes that on one of these looks it will be full of delicious cold cuts of meat, leftover roast potatoes and Black Forest gateaux.

The fridge is still empty. Proceed to plan B.

Take two slices of bread. Find clean knife to butter bread.

Realise someone has put butter back in fridge and now it's too cold to spread. Hack at cold butter in a futile fashion for at least five minutes, cutting off tiny scrapes and/or huge wodges and trying to spread them onto the bread.

Tear big hole in bread. This bread is now not suitable for the recipe. Eat holey slice with some raspberry jam. Do not fret, as the extra bread we eat while making meals is sometimes the most delicious thing of all.

Admit defeat with the butter situation. Decide to microwave a portion of butter for four to five seconds to make it spreadable.

Frown at the baked bean stalactites hanging from the roof of the microwave and remind yourself that you should really get round to cleaning this thing at some point. This year, in an ideal world.

Replace eaten slice of bread. Butter both slices with newly softened butter.

Turn on stove to medium heat.

Take third piece of bread. Cut crusts off to ensure it is smaller than the other two pieces. Feel guilty about not eating the crusts. Find yourself wishing you were the type of person with time to make one of those *Blue Peter* bird feeders so crusts would not go to waste. Admit that you aren't.

Cut off another few inches of butter and place in pan. When it is melted and golden, pop in the crustless piece of bread. Fry it in the butter, turning occasionally until the bread is golden and crisp and utterly irresistible.

Take bread from pan, turn off heat, place fried bread on top of one of the pieces of buttered bread.

Add brown sauce in a Jackson Pollock spatter effect. (Other abstract expressionist painters are available.)

Place the other piece of buttered bread on top of the sauce to create sandwich. I will not insult you by further explaining how a sandwich works: you've got this.

Cut sandwich. (NB: Jo Brand did not cut hers at all, instead opting to pick the whole thing up, and ate a large bite out of the corner – I'm calling this 'chaotic'. Personally, I feel this sandwich lends itself to a diagonal cut, which provides better access to the butter, and it also allows you to monitor for any dry parts; add further brown sauce where necessary.)

Eat sandwich immediately while conducting a post-mortem of the evening with friends on WhatsApp; this must include input from that one friend who can track down any random you snogged within about thirty-seven seconds as if they're in *CSI: Crime Scene Investigation*.

Feel remarkably rosier about life. Bring small snuggly duvet onto sofa. Realise that Gold channel is playing *Gavin and Stacey* season one from the beginning. Settle in. Today is going to be a good day.

Uncomfortable Eating

Not all eating is comfortable. In fact, some of it is just plain arduous. Here, I identify the worst culprits:

Green pepper

In small amounts, the green pepper is not offensive, but let's be honest: it is absolutely nobody's favourite pepper in the 'red–orange–green' pepper pack. Red is the favourite, orange is its tolerated second-best sister, and green is the third wheel at the party. Put it this way: when you order chicken in black bean sauce from the takeaway, you get three pieces of chicken, yes, but you also get a box of virtually raw green pepper doing the backstroke in the sauce, ruining your Friday as you pick around it. See also: ruined fajitas, pasta salad and the dismal veggie option on any barbecue. Uncomfortable Eating Rating: 4/10

Quinoa

Pronounced 'KE-NUH-WAH' and not 'QUINN-OH-AH' – that's your first mistake, as the person taking your order laughs down their sleeve and runs to the kitchen to announce they've got another uncultured fool in who'd be happier down at Toby Inn. Sure, quinoa is a good idea for many reasons: it's healthy, it's low-carb, it's versatile and you can whizz it up in minutes in a fast-cooker. However, it does taste like damp sand. No matter what you hurl at quinoa, be it butter, oil, salt, herbs or garlic, you will still eat every mouthful of it thinking, 'I wish this was delicious, buttered basmati rice.' Uncomfortable Eating Rating: 5/10

Spores

Oh, crust of bread! Your saviour! The cupboards are bare and all you need is a little something-something to line your tummy before bed. Toast and Marmite, toast and jam, toast and . . . MOULD SPORES?! You spot green out of your right eye, coming towards you as you're halfway through chomping. Do you stop eating? No. But during those last few bites you feel like Bear Grylls. Uncomfortable Eating Rating: 6/10

Pre-soak pulses

Mung beans, urad dal, adzuki beans: nothing is more comforting than a delicious dal or something hearty with chickpeas, and believe me when I say that I could write an entire love letter to the versatility of pre-canned black beans. But here I'm talking about that moment when, shortly after getting the pots and pans out and chopping the onion and grating the ginger, you realise you were meant to begin TWELVE HOURS AGO. 'Not a problem,' you think. 'I'll cook this stew tomorrow.' You fill a large bowl with several litres of water, begin soaking the pigeon peas . . . and then promptly forget them for seventy-two hours. They have swelled to the size of golf balls, and you must put them in the bin. Oh dear oh dear. Uncomfortable Eating Rating: 6/10

Rocket salad

From June onwards in Britain anyone hoping for a 'nice refreshing salad' should stay extra vigilant for roquette, the peppery, bitter leaf with a scratchy surface that is bound to ruin any al fresco eating. Nobody in the UK ate roquette until about 1996, when, much like Jamiroquai and bootcut jeans, it became unavoidable. Until then, we were content with iceberg lettuce or, if we were being truly fancy, something curly-leaved and safe, served with Heinz salad cream and hard-boiled egg. Then, suddenly, BAM, roquette was everywhere, sitting beside your chicken Kiev in the pub, as welcoming as a patch of stinging nettles. Don't even get me started on its cruel stepsister, 'endive'. Just say no. Uncomfortable Eating Level: 6/10

Half a grapefruit

Ah yes, the sophisticated but ultimately depressing breakfast choice. If you've ever stayed in the type of fancy hotel that lets you pre-order room service breakfast, you'll find 'half a grapefruit' on the long list of tick boxes on the card that you must place on your door before 2 a.m. (it's always 2 a.m., don't ask why). The list is always a tempting cornucopia of pastries, toast baskets, full English, full-cream porridge, and boiled eggs and soldiers. 'Oh no, I must be good,' you think, imagining that it's choices like this that have led Joan Collins to look sprightlier aged ninety than you do at thirty-one. So you order the grapefruit and it arrives, and it's bitter and a little hard, and the first spoonful of it unleashes juice directly into your eyeball. Who are you kidding? You'll buy a Greggs Sausage, Bean

& Cheese Melt shortly after checkout. Uncomfortable Eating Rating: 7/10

The artichoke heart

Of all the difficult foods to be presented with at a 'fancy' restaurant, I must warn you of the artichoke heart, green, bulbous and covered in petals. Oh, it looks so pretty on the plate, there with its delightful mayo and Parmesan dip. Aren't you adventurous for ordering it. Aren't you healthy. So how do you actually eat it? No one is sure. Don't attempt to cut it with a knife and fork – you'll need a Black + Decker strimmer to make an impact on this beast. Begin by ripping off the petals with your hands, which seems most logical, naturally. The edible part of the leaf is the 0.3 mm of slightly squishy leaf at the centre. Do not push the whole leaf into your mouth (please refer back to p. 39 in the cheese chapter for further details on public choking in a room full of posh people). After completing one leaf, carry on to the next, nibbling the tiny squirrel's teacup full of 'food' on each one, while everyone else at the table enjoys prawn cocktail, deep-fried breadcrumbed mushrooms and the starters that you wish you'd ordered. Uncomfortable Eating Rating: 7/10

Breakfast in a tin

Comfort Eating – both the podcast and the lifestyle choice – heavily endorses delicious things in cans: spaghetti, rice pudding, baked beans, you name it. A line is drawn, however, at the tinned all-day breakfast, which gives even the most ardent supporter of the grocery aisle at the twenty-four-hour Esso garage the rampant heebie-jeebies. Pre-cooked sausages, rashers of bacon, fried mushrooms, 'pork and egg nuggets', scrambled egg – the contents vary from brand to brand, but it's safe to say any formulation resembles a crime scene more than a delicious breakfast. It plops out of the can as a congealed lump of unrecognisable meaty bits, resembling something found in a serial killer's fridge. AVOID AVOID AVOID. Uncomfortable Eating Rating: 8/10

Toblerone

The British are compelled to purchase a large Toblerone while walking through any airport, just as our ancestors did, and their ancestors before them. For as long as people have packed Ambre Solaire tanning oil and budgie smugglers and waved goodbye to their street for ten nights, all-inclusive, in Lloret de Mar, Spain, we have brought back extra-large Toblerone – which is in fact a taste of Switzerland, but that's not the point. Toblerone back in the seventies and eighties was never about where you'd been on holiday, it was about the glamour of air travel and the bargains to be had at duty-free. At the end of a journey, you'll crack it open and realise the individual 'mountains' in the bar are only edible if you relax your jaw like a northern Peruvian boa constrictor attempting to eat a wild javelina pig. Uncomfortable Eating Rating: 8/10

Andouillette sausage

Nothing in the *Tricolore* textbook prepares you for andouillette sausage, the intestines of a pig minced so roughly that the tubes are still recognisable and the colon-adjacent parts are giving off a shamelessly detectable whiff of lavatory. The French love it, and the French love it when we accidentally order it. 'Haha-ha, silly rosbifs, how you like Brexit now?' they laugh as you struggle to swallow some of the knobblier part of Babe the pig's larger intestine. Just don't bother. I mean it. Uncomfortable Eating Rating: 9/10

POTATOES

. . . And Why They're Proof of a Higher Power

Birds Eye potato waffles,
They're waffly versatile.
They go with cheese, chilli, chicken, burgers, fish fingers,
   a-fish fingers!
Eggs in, eggs on, gammon, lamb chop.
Grill 'em, bake 'em, fry 'em, eat 'em.
Birds Eye potato waffles,
They're waffly versatile!

Potatoes are pretty strong evidence that there's a God, if you ask me. They're proof that there's *something* up there, rooting for our survival. They'll grow anywhere there's a patch of muck – from Margate to Mexico City – saving our mortal souls from starvation. If there is a benevolent, all-seeing higher power floating around, I can taste it in a large Maris Piper potato, peeled, then chopped into chunks, parboiled until slightly softened and hurled into something fatty before finally being roasted. God is there in that crispy roast potato, stuck ever so slightly to the baking tray, fluffy in the middle, crunchy on the surface and the corners (and the best roasties do have corners). I love to pop a roast potato in my mouth when I am supposed to be dishing up Sunday lunch for other people, sprinkled with extra sea salt and dipped into the gravy boat before it's whisked to the table. And then, on a cold Monday, warmed-up roast spuds eaten in bed will speak directly to your soul. They'll say: everything is OK.

Or even more heavenly still: bubble and squeak with mashed leftover roasties. Just a gently fried onion and some of the shredded leftover Sunday green things: cabbage, Brussels, peas. 'Bubble', as they call it in London caffs, to my mind, should be peppery. But not with fancy black pepper ground from a proper grinder. No, this time it must be that thin, grey, already ground pepper that comes in a white plastic cylinder that my dad put on everything in the seventies. This abrasive heat goes beautifully with the balm-like spud. Serve bubble and squeak topped with a crispy-bottomed fried egg with runny yolk and a large dash of something hot, red and spicy like Sriracha or Japanese chili oil. Drag a blanket around you on the sofa and catch up on *Coronation Street*. Yes, suffering is a natural part of our earthly existence, and everything we love is fragile, but potatoes make this all more tolerable.

Admittedly, the potato in its natural form would not win a beauty contest. It is knobbly, often sludge-coloured and sometimes whiskery: all words that I would use to describe myself in the 'between' times when I'm not hurling money at beauticians. Maybe I identify with potatoes so much because they are, without titivation, an absolute five in the looks department. I have thought often about Sir Walter Raleigh pitching up at Portsmouth with his cargo of 'discoveries' to impress Queen Elizabeth, and how the potato must have been a particularly hard sell. Who could get excited about this bulbous lump with a thin, bitter skin which could only be removed with a sharp knife to reveal raw innards that tasted of gritty nothingness?

But people *did* get excited: spuds are eaten in their billions all over the world. I know this for certain following a question which saw me crash out of an episode of the BBC1 game show *Pointless*, a moment I still have mild PTSD about (for more on this, see the crisp section later on). They love them in Iran, Pakistan, Poland, Russia and even in France, where they're really very picky about foods; don't call a chip a French fry there, however – they don't like that at all. They are very proud of their *pommes boulangère*, though, where thin layers of spuds are stewed in stock with leek to create something quite heavenly. Miraculous things happen when you give a potato some love. The grittiness turns to sweetness and fluffiness; that bitter skin becomes delicious when baked to a crisp. Potatoes are an undeniable comfort food, and when you show them affection with fat, heat and salt, they perk up and love you right back.

On the podcast, potatoes come up time and again as something the stars reach for when the, ahem, chips are down. Pun intended. Comedian and former *Strictly Come Dancing* star Jade Adams actually made her own chips to her own special recipe: big chunks of Maris Piper rolled in crumbled Oxo cubes, shallow fried in a pan and served with fried Spam. Jade's *Comfort Eating* interview was completely from the heart; she covered the death of her sister, her painful school years and much more, all while ploughing through a large plate of those chips, and it was nothing short of majestic to watch.

Another comedian, Munya Chawawa, admitted, just a little sheepishly, that after another punishing day of absolutely ruling social media with his satirical skits, he asks Deliveroo to order his favourite Nando's: a side of 'creamy and comforting' mash and a side of grilled pineapple. Yes, that's the entire order. No main, just sides. No butterfly chicken burger or double chicken pitta with peri-peri hot sauce. Munya just wants the mash, and when he orders the restaurant does try to call him to see if there's been an error, which there definitely hasn't been. This is just a man who knows what he wants.

Author and presenter Dawn O'Porter went for a double spud combo on her episode: Marks & Spencer's luxury potato salad with thick-cut salt and vinegar crisps scooped through. I spoke to her over Zoom as she was in Los Angeles writing a novel while her husband Chris O'Dowd filmed yet another Holly-wood blockbuster. Dawn and Chris are great entertainers, never happier than when their house is full of guests to feed (they often have Kristen Wiig and Jason Segel round to eat a traditional Irish Sunday roast). Personally, I get a stress migraine think-ing about all those hungry faces and all that expectation, not to mention the task of finding Bisto gravy granules on the Sunset Strip, but Dawn is something of a powerhouse, so she can han-dle it. Her crisp/potato salad snack, she told me, was something she invented while cooking, because the chef often doesn't get to eat properly as they're too busy fiddling with pans.

Marks's food hall does tend to come up on the *Comfort Eat-ing* podcast rather a lot – probably because for a lot of British people it's still seen as a cut above the other supermarkets, as somewhere where you pick up 'picky bits' for a treat, or where you get the fancier items at Christmas. I fondly remember their potato salad with chives being a once-a-year thing for Boxing Day tea in the eighties: so decadent! Clearly this was some-thing duchesses and lords ate with their roasted swan, washing it down with champagne. Or, in my case, my dad had it with his pork pie, pairing it with a bottle of Newcastle Brown Ale while wearing a wonky Christmas hat – but more on that later.

———

Potato was one of the very first words I said. Well, almost. I actually said 'Smmmmmmaaaaaash'. And not long after that, perhaps only weeks later, I sang the entire seventies Smash advert's slogan: 'For maaaaash get Smaaaaaash'. Smash was, and still is to this day, dried reconstituted mashed potato that comes in a canister in the form of pellets. You can pick it up and rattle it like a makeshift maraca if you so wish. In the seventies this was supposed to be the answer for harassed mothers trying to get food on the table quickly. No need for peeling or chopping or carrying heavy bags of spuds back from Presto, just shove it into a bowl and add boiling water, then mix to create what was honestly a greying mush.

But as a little girl I loved Smash, and I still rather like it now. There's a canister in my cupboard as part of my emotional first aid kit. It reminds of me of my childhood days, of simplicity, of a time before everything became fast and hectic and complex. It catapults me back to the lovely slow crapness of life before the internet, when there were only three channels on the telly and a BT landline in the vestibule for emergencies. I loved Smash's claggy texture; it was almost like edible playdough, and if Mam added too much water to loosen it, it would end up turning into a sort of wallpaper paste.

And I loved the advert with the aliens who are having a meeting about stupid humans on planet Earth who still think actual real potatoes are worth wasting time on. The ad finishes with a round of electrified alien laughing, which by seventies standards was very exciting. In my highchair, as a tiny tot, I learned to recite it. This ad campaign was genius: my mother was tired; she had a lot on her plate with two toddlers and a teenager. She was definitely sick of being tied to that blunt seventies spud peeler with the coloured string-bound handle. Smash was the answer. I ate it readily, no quibble: I ate it with ketchup, I ate it with salad cream, I ate it with spaghetti hoops, I ate it dry out of the packet when she wasn't looking. The main thing I learned from Smash, however, is that cutting corners with potatoes does not improve them. The best potatoes need time.

My true love affair with the potato began in the late seventies due to our neighbour on Harold Street, Mrs Latham, who used to throw spuds over our back wall. We lived at no. 21, she was at no. 19. Oh, Mrs Latham, with her little dog Trixie the poodle, or a 'poodle cross' as Mrs Latham would always say when the chubby little thing was mentioned. Crossed with what exactly we had no idea, but Trixie had a delicate, fluffy face and curly ears, though by the time you got around the stomach area she was more like a Staffordshire bull terrier. Trixie was famous down our street for being highly intelligent because she knew the words 'ball', 'walk' and 'biscuit', tearing around the flag-stones when she heard them in passing conversation.

Living in a terraced street doesn't give you a lot of privacy. You might not be able to see your neighbours, but you can often hear them. Our house's back yard was divided from Mrs Latham's yard by a thin brick wall. When me and David played outside, by the bins, I could hear her in her kitchen and smell the Madeira cake or rock buns she was baking for one bake sale or another. Mrs Latham was a good egg: she never complained when we banged tennis balls off her window by accident, or when me and my friends Tracey, Jenny and Pamela set up a Sindy camping trip on her back step. And looking back, she really did have cause to complain: Harold Street had a child or two or three in almost every house. On the long summer holidays we played outside from dawn to dusk, sliding about on roller skates, playing Stan and British Bulldog and cadging our teas at each other's houses. In the back lane, which was basically a dirt track, our favourite game was to dig up the dirt in buckets, add water and make our own mud. Mrs Latham put up with Ian Dury's 'Hit Me with Your Rhythm Stick' being played twenty times a day and the sound of my Mam screaming with fury because me and David had scaled the side of our other neighbour Billie Marshall's coal lorry again. We could not resist the challenge of climbing the mesh up the side of it, with half a dozen other kids. It was the best of childhoods, it was the worst of childhoods, depending on how you look at it.

When I asked my brother, forty years later, if he remembered Mrs Latham at all, he thought for a long time and said, 'Miss Marple. That's all I've got.' He can see the tweed skirts and the smart cardigans and the fleece-like white hair, but that's it. He doesn't remember that she made her own tipsy cake, nor the sound of her and my Mam rabbiting away on the back step in Cumberland dialect – a language that is almost lost now – about someone unwell who 'wonnt in ower grand fettle', or, even worse, was 'deed'. Someone being 'deed' (dead) on Harold Street was very exciting. One of the mams would have to hold us captive while the undertakers got the body out. David remembers none of this. And he absolutely does not remember the over-the-wall potatoes.

This all came about as Mrs Latham did not like waste. Any

leftover scrap of ham hock or bacon rind went to Trixie, and if there was spare space on a rack in her oven, she cooked something for someone else too. Mam explained to me many times that old folks were weird about wasting stuff like eggs, sugar or gas because of a big war that happened about thirty years back – a war our Grandad fought in. All this luxury we had, Mam said, casting her hand around the sheer opulence of our terrace with its rubber mixer shower attachment and posh peach melba Ski yoghurts in the fridge, should not be taken for granted. Old people know how to be frugal, she told me, and it was this frugality that led one of my most life-enhancing food experiences: my very first oven-baked jacket potato.

I can still taste it if I close my eyes. It's a Saturday morning and I've been forewarned while settling down to watch *Tiswas* on Border TV that Mrs Latham has a special treat for me. I can already smell the gas of the oven floating over the wall, and what I think might be a pie going in with mincemeat, or a batch of scones. *Tiswas* goes on for ever, a riot of cartoons and silly adults chucking custard pies and a man called Lenny Henry shouting 'ooooooooookkkkkkkkkkkkay' and pop stars being put in cages and soaked with water. My mother does not approve of *Tiswas*, but it keeps me out of her hair as she irons and sews on school badges and loads the washing machine and pays the insurance man and gives in to my moaning for a glass of banana Nesquik.

As the clock creeps to midday, Mrs Latham comes to her back door and shouts for my Mam. Mam stands up and rushes out clutching a posh Harrods tea towel. Mrs Latham is on tiptoes – I can just see the curls of her hair – and she starts to fling the potatoes over the wall for my Mam to catch, both of them laughing like mad. Mam brings the treasure inside: three jacket potatoes wrapped in tin foil, warm and gorgeous-smelling. Mam unwraps the foil and slits them open, then mashes the insides with margarine until they are golden, then sprinkles with salt. The flesh is cloudlike and the skin crispy. Sometimes Mam opens a tin of beans to serve with them and sometimes she grates some Cheddar. But this first time, we eat the potatoes with just marge and salt. Immediately I loved that scratchy, crispy skin, which it felt weirdly brave to eat, like we were doing something very unnatural, and most of all, I loved those forkfuls of potato where the spud-to-marge ratio had tipped too far into the marge zone. For those fabulous moments as it slid down my throat, life was much more radiant than it had ever been before.

I was hooked.

(As an aside, about six years later – after Mrs Latham had died and we inherited Trixie the poodle cross, and after I was too much of a big girl for things like *Tiswas* and would only watch *Going Live* on Saturday mornings in case a kid rang in and told Five Star they were shit – the microwave oven entered the Dent household. The pamphlet that came with this amazing space-age device told us in German, Japanese and thankfully English that there was an exciting, fresh method to make jacket spuds: simply place a potato on the glass plate and blast it with electro-magnetic radiation for about eight minutes! A delicious meal in moments, it promised. This was a lie. Show me a Generation X teenager and I will show you someone who has eaten a withered lump of spud with papery skin that spat at them through the fork holes. Or someone who tried to eat that rock-hard patch of skin that had rested on the glass plate, half-choking as it tangled round their teeth. God is not present in a microwaved jacket potato. It is a product of Satan.)

'Susan, 36–22–35, loves going out with her friends to disco-theques and staying home doing jigsaw puzzles. I think a few viewers will be thinking that by the look of her in this swimsuit . . . she's got all the pieces in the right place! That's number 9 . . . MISS ENGLAND!'

In the early eighties my family took the *Miss World* show on BBC1 very seriously. We took our plates of McCain oven chips and beans to the couch, along with scraps of notepaper with which we'd cast our own votes on the girls, judging their hair, their smiles and the slinkiness of their bottoms. It was both terrifically exciting and wildly scarring for me, all at the same time. There was an evening dress round and a bikini round and a chance for women to prove their pleasant personality by chatting live on stage with the greasy man who invented the competition called Eric Morley. He would say that contestants had to be between seventeen and twenty-five, ideally five foot seven and weighting eight or nine stone, with a waist between twenty-two and twenty-four inches and hips between thirty-five and thirty-six inches, no more no less. Oh, and on top of that, they had to have a lovely face, good teeth, plenty of hair and 'perfectly shaped legs from front and back'.

I would never go on to fulfil any of Eric's requirements. Aged ten, however, I still had hope. These measurements they read out on screen became fixated in my brain: the first number was the boobs, the second the waist, the third the hips. 'The hourglass', I heard it called. At that point my body was more like a bulbous lump with little fat thighs. As I reached my late teens, I developed a small waist and a bigger bust, but this merely accentuated my hips, which were always more like thirty-nine inches. Sometimes bigger.

What sticks in my mind from when I still had my dream of walking across the stage on BBC1 wearing a sparkly crown and a sash was an important lesson I learned: beauty queens shouldn't eat potatoes. Beauty queens avoid eating starchy carbs, which I was very quickly learning was a real shame, because 'starchy carbs' must be some of the most beautiful, evocative words in the English language. Eating starchy carbs means you know you're about to be full. Gorgeously, generously full.

This lesson could also be found in my Mam's *Woman's Own* magazines, which gave tips for ladies wishing to 'win some admiring glances' in summer, and I read similar things in the *Slimming World* magazines she kept in piles on the bottom rung of the coffee table, along with diet plans torn out from every tabloid newspaper – we used them on our knees when the plates were too hot. Not one of these plans included chips, mashed spuds, potato waffles or lovely roasties. These diets sometimes included 'three small new potatoes, no butter, no oil', or said things like 'why not try swapping potato for something lighter, like radishes or cucumber?' At ten years old I may not yet have been a food expert, but even I knew radishes and potatoes were not the same thing. Or potatoes and cucumber slices. Or potatoes and two tablespoons of low-fat chive-flavoured cottage cheese. Nobody has ever swapped potato waffles for undressed iceberg lettuce and felt cheerier.

As I got older, though, I sadly (and often) lived without potatoes as I joined Mam on her diets. It always felt like the sun going in and a long winter of the soul beginning. Her starving on three small meals a day, me participating partly for moral support and partly as I too was feeling somewhat imperfect. This time, we told ourselves, we would look like beauty queens, her like Krystle Carrington off *Dynasty* and me like Linda Lusardi from page three in the *Sun*. The purge would go on for around five days, and we'd grimly subsist on dry Ryvitas and boiled eggs, avoiding the chips at Wimpy and my daily mint Aero and pre-bed Mr Kipling apple pies at all costs. By Friday we would both be half mad with starvation and she would get on the scales and announce that she hadn't lost 'a single solitary ounce'!

And then Dad would mention the words that still bring joy to hear – something much bigger than my urge to look like a beauty queen.

'Chippy tea?' he'd say.

'Go and get me purse,' Mam would reply. The curse was broken.

The greatest chippy teas of my entire life were from Donny's, in Currock. As I walk through life I am always searching for those chips, for that blissful mood, for that hazy joy those chips provoked. I want to feel the thrill of finding extra bonus chips that have slipped between layers of the *Cumberland News*; I want to recreate the furtive joy of shoving them into my gob, even though I'm supposed to be making mine and my little brother's plates equal. I want the companionable silence of my family devouring them. This is what I want from chip-shop chips. The quality of the oil and the fluffiness of the chip's inner are almost unimportant. I want the feeling of a chippy tea itself.

Donny's was a small, white-tiled fish and chip shop at the Five Road Ends roundabout. I was dispatched to Donny's alone many times from infant-school age. Or to the newsagent, the Co-op, the bookie, the chemist, the veg shop, or even to take a message from Dad to Ray the midnight barber who cut hair till late for people coming back off the 2–10 p.m. shift at Carr's biscuit factory. It feels odd now that folk sent infant-school children across main roads on errands, but it was all perfectly normal and no one ever died – although, OK, there were a lot of very near misses.

Donny's itself was a brightly lit, amazing-smelling place, with steamy windows and a queue that often snaked out of the door. Donny himself was always standing behind the counter wearing a pristine white coat, as if he worked in a laboratory. He was about six foot tall with short, quiffed silvery hair and piercing blue eyes. All the mams in Currock had a soft spot for Donny, which as a little girl I thought was very weird, because he was a very old man, of at least forty. Now I can see why. He was funny, handsome and a ready supplier of beige, starchy carbs, the most delicious food group of all.

My favourite times going to the chippy were when I walked there with Dad. It was a little bit of me and him time. Working-class dads in the eighties did not take their daughters to a whole lot of places. Bonding exercises just weren't a thing: he didn't encourage me to support his team, Liverpool FC, or teach me how to shoot a gun or fix a car, all of which he was very good at. However, I still think of our trips to the chip shop fondly, and I can still feel the thrill of the shop itself. Packed on a Friday night, Donny taking orders and transferring chips from the hot fryer into the large drum beside it, and one of the local lasses shovelling them directly onto paper, not into a polystyrene carton, shaking salt from a white plastic shaker and sploshing brown malt vinegar over them. People in the queue would shout out their orders so Donny knew what needed to be stuck in the fryer, ready for them by the time they reached the front. There was a system in this madness!

'Three fish, Donny!' someone would shout.

'Have you got a battered haggis?' someone else would say. Carlisle, being near the border of Scotland, needed to cater to the sophisticated tastes of our foreign neighbours. Donny would disappear into a room at the back where the rumbling, chundering chipping machine lived, and soon he'd return to hurl a frozen haggis into the oil. Donny also did 'white pudding' for the Scots, made of suet, oatmeal and pork liver. The Dents never went for anything as flamboyant as this: our order was usually something like three portions of chips, two large fish and sometimes a sausage or a steak pie for one of us kids. The pinnacle of chippy foods, for me, was the 'patty', which is peculiar to Cumberland: battered, deep-fried mashed potato with beef mince, spherical in shape, like a tennis ball. Patties were heaven to me. They still are heaven to me.

By the time we were ordering, all thought of diets and low-calorie, high-fibre plans had left my mind. That could all start again on Monday, or next month, with depressing regularity for the rest of my life. But not now. Right now, in this moment, I'm living my very best life. If we were lucky, we'd get a portion of 'scraps' added to the order, the leftover batter scrapings that Donny hid in a secret compartment and doled out to regulars. Me and Dad would walk home as quickly as we could, me eating a pickled egg out of a paper bag with a warning not to tell my little brother as he'd only moan it wasn't fair. At home, Mam would have plates and forks out. We never ate from newspaper on our knees. We weren't 'common': we had pebble dash on our house and everything!

The best chips, I know for sure, are the ones you snatch for yourself as you are dividing them up for you and your brothers at the kitchen counter. This offers the most giddy high. The next five to ten minutes are ecstasy, as soft, squashy chip-shop chips glide down our throats, taking our cares away. My little stomach filling, no longer hungry, no longer caring about having chunky thighs in summer shorts like one of the nasty boys in the street pointed out. No longer caring about that. Just happy. As we become fuller and a little bloated, the chips cooling, our plates almost empty, we become a little less enamoured with them, until eventually someone will always give up eating and say: 'Oh, I am stuffed, does anyone want any of my chips?' And in that moment, the magic is broken. The real world, with its beauty queens in sashes and waists where you can't pinch more than an inch, creeps back in. Until the next time. And there will always be a next time.

But how does any of this prove the existence of a higher power? Well, potatoes have saved my life so many times. And yours too, perhaps. The joyous nature of the spud is ever reliable, *especially* on those mornings when you wake up in a low-budget chain hotel to the 7.23 a.m. alarm you set on your phone, having set the first two directly to snooze. This was an error. You are now in the danger zone. That train you said you'd be up to catch, that meeting with the company bigwig you're here for, that presentation you said you'd give, that friend's wedding you should already be ironing for – all those things that seem very noble when you promise to do them – are looming large.

And now it's 7.28 a.m. and you're still in bed and you're hating being a grown-up. Under your surprisingly cosy duvet, in a room that really could be anywhere in Britain given that every low-budget hotel room is identikit, a bleakness about the day has set in. Last night's dinner was two glasses of white wine and a Greggs Yum Yum you bought in a service station, which was delicious but not a balanced meal in any sense of the term. In the middle of the night, on the way to the loo, after tripping over the purple Premier Inn sash that was over the top of the duvet, you got back into bed and ate two complimentary Lotus biscuits in the dark. You are starving.

And here, in your hotel room, at 7.36 a.m., you begin to wonder, what is this all about? This life? All you've achieved is working hard in a job you don't particularly like, to pay off credit card debts for things to make you marginally happier, with your free time cluttered up by responsibilities like council tax demands, remembering bin days, collecting missing parcels from the depot and finding places to hang damp clothes so they don't go mildewy. What is the point in being on planet Earth at all?

There is a small chance you are being dramatic.

Here is where the holy power of potatoes will heal you.

It is now 7.41 a.m. A small sliver of hope enters your brain in the form of a vague smell.

It isn't necessarily a very nice smell; it's a nondescript fatty smell, but a welcome smell nevertheless, a smell reminiscent of chip pans and coffee machines, of school dinner halls and service stations. This is the smell of 'catering', and it means something very wonderful. Breakfast has opened! Hotel breakfast! You recall the magical words the receptionist said as she gave you the key card: 'Breakfast is included with your room and it begins at 7 a.m. It's a serve-yourself buffet; just follow the signs.'

Some of the sweetest noises in the English language: breakfast. Buffet.

You begin throwing on clothes quickly, anything that will make you acceptable to the human eye at this time. Baggy sweatshirts, comfy bottoms. If you are British-born, you pray there are no other human beings present at the buffet. Part of the UK citizenship test should possibly contain the question: 'Would you rather stab yourself to death with a blunt butter knife than talk to a fellow hotel guest who is waiting for some toast in the big whirly communal toaster?' The breakfast buffet is not a social occasion. It is a solemn, pious one.

And now you're walking down a maze of corridors in your low-budget hotel, noticing, in the light of day, that it's on a three-lane roundabout in an industrial estate. You're staggering zombie-like towards the smell. That smell. The smell of beige refined-carb items. Yes, there will be packets of Weetabix and that awful bowl of partially frozen mixed berries, but you don't want that. The heart wants what it wants. It wants the thing that will take the pain away, the thing that will make your stomach feel attended to. It wants those things in the silver terrine that sit beside those weird little overcooked sausages, next to mushrooms swimming in grease and the terrifying scrambled eggs. Your heart wants hash browns. Delicious, crispy, golden hash browns.

You spot them lying under a lamp that keeps them warm, and like a majestic golden eagle flying over its terrain, you swoop, and you are victorious. These hash browns are cooked expertly. They were taken from a walk-in freezer and chucked into an oven, several hours ago, by whichever poor sod was stuck with the breakfast shift at Premier Inn Slough. The chef is now standing at the back of the hotel, smoking a Winston Red, cursing their own existence. Why are they up at 5 a.m. to cook hash browns? What is the meaning of *their* life?

This hero, in sacrificing their sanity, has restored yours. The hash browns are abundant, they're hot and they're crispy. The mundane details of adult life won't matter when you load them onto your plate alongside one of those very hard-yolked fried eggs, drizzling baked beans over the lot. You find a table for one in the breakfast room with your back to everyone, lest anyone even try to smile at you. It is 7.45 a.m. You have ten whole minutes to yourself. You begin loading the exquisite, greasy, salty hash browns into your face, barely chewing, barely breathing, sanity restoring, stomach filling, hope flooding back.

This private moment puts you back on track. Just you and your sumptuous, healing hash brown breakfast. Just you and your lovely plate of reconstituted potato with non-hydrogenated vegetable oil mixed with diphosphate stabilising powder.

All carb, virtually no dietary fibre and not a trace of vitamins: absolutely no regrets.

Today is going to be fine.

Confession: crisps are one of my biggest downfalls, and although I have made a point during the course of this book never to decry any food as naughty or evil or blame it for anything, when it comes to crisps, I have some fingers to point. Crisps are just too damn delicious. If I have them in the house, I eat them instantly, eschewing all other food; being starving hungry and then shovelling crisps down your throat is probably one of life's greatest and most base joys. I am simply powerless.

Crisps are one of the twentieth century's greatest culinary inventions: portable, filling, comforting and available in a thousand different flavours. My personal Achilles' heel of snacking is Walkers pickled onion crisps . . . or Seabrook Worcestershire sauce . . . or Tyrrells smoked paprika. Oh, the crinkle of the packet, the whiff as you inhale the flavouring, the tingling of your tastebuds preparing for this overload of potato joy! My love is ancient and passionate and overpowering. I cannot add crisps to my grocery delivery on a casual basis. My love for them is not casual, particularly when it comes to sweet chilli crisps. These are perfect in a voluminous layer across the bottom of a cheese sandwich (or an egg sandwich or a ham sandwich or a jam sandwich for that matter), and better still when eaten in bed in the comfiest of pyjamas on a wintery Saturday while watching a period drama starring Matthew Macfadyen in well-packed jodhpurs.

The very finest crisps, however, may well be that mini packet of complimentary crisps they hand out on aeroplanes when you're going on holiday. The packet only contains about five crisps but they're always incredibly fresh due to the high turnover in passengers, and they pair beautifully with a cold diet Coke and a shufty through the in-flight catalogue that houses Britney Spears's line of perfume gifts and Ferrero Rocher prestige gift boxes. Bliss. Some of my happiest times on holiday are those moments when you get back from the beach, take a shower, nap and then eat some fancy foreign crisps with a glass of fizzy stuff on your balcony. Herr's Creamy Dill Pickle Ridge-Backed! Zapp's Voodoo New Orleans Kettle-Style! Let me ride the rollercoaster of flavourings!

Although I'm more careful about my home-based crisp consumption, I can never resist the ones they leave me in the dressing room at TV studios. They're meant to be a little snack before you go on set, though in my case they're usually something to console me after I've made a colossal berk of myself (again) on another TV game show. My most memorable pack of TV studio crisps was probably the one I ate on the way home from Elstree after crashing out of the BBC1 show *Pointless* with William Sitwell. We were the first duo to leave, and it was due to a question about potatoes. God was not smiling down at me via spuds on this day. This particular *Pointless* episode was a food special, and in the green room beforehand Dame Prue Leith was hobnobbing with chef Brian Turner CBE, chef Michael Caines MBE and others who constituted the great and good of the culinary world. The atmosphere was very competitive, with everyone clearly determined to win . . . aside from myself, who, to be honest, did not really understand how *Pointless* worked.

'But you've been on the show before!' said William.

'Yes, I know, and I didn't understand it last time!' I hissed. 'I just shouted words and got lucky.' At this point William's face went rather white, and then we were led to our podiums.

The beginning of the show went rather well, and I answered all of Alexander Armstrong's questions correctly, but sadly I soon realised that this was before the actual game had begun, and the questions were just asking things like my name and where I worked. Things quickly got trickier: we were asked to name a country that was in the world's top ten when it came to the highest annual potato harvests.

You could probably have a good go at guessing this answer yourself, but nothing on *Pointless* is straightforward – to stay in the game you must guess an answer that, while correct, must also be an unpopular answer that no one else said. Are you with me so far? Probably not, because *Pointless* is a horrible game show designed to make you very confused and panicked, especially when you're surrounded by celebrities and a camera is on your face and you cannot think of a single country that even eats potatoes, not even Ireland. The silence was deafening – and then William shouted, 'NEW ZEALAND!' The buzzer went *BZZZZZZZZZZZZZZ* and we were kicked off and sent home.

I walked back to the dressing room with tears in my eyes and picked up a packet of Walkers salt and vinegar crisps that had been put in a little gift basket. I opened them, inhaled the vinegary fumes and fed them into my face, one by one. They reminded me of home, of Carlisle, of my Mam, of trips to the shops with coppers that I'd found down the back of the sofa. They also tasted of revenge . . . Potatoes had slayed me and now I would devour them. Inanimate starch-based objects, they would not be the boss of me.

Anyway. In a world of endless crisp choice, I still have plenty of love for ready salted. Yes, some people think it's boring, or even sinister, but this was my entry-level crisp, the start of my love. Back in the seventies, 'salt' was really the only flavour crisps came in, and this wasn't even 'ready' salted. No, all Gen X kids remember a time when the most popular crisps sold down the local off licence were Smiths Salt 'n' Shake. This was a white bag filled with genuinely unflavoured crisps, and within this white bag, very excitingly, was a small blue sachet about as big as a postage stamp filled with salt. You had to sprinkle the salt on the crisps yourself before scrunching the bag up and jumping around to disperse it; I remember doing this to the song 'Making Your Mind Up' by Bucks Fizz, though I'm sure other pop songs work just as well. Bizarrely, Walkers still make Salt 'n' Shake crisps today, which I find a comfort all on its own. I am soothed by the thought that in this hyper-stimulated world, there are some people out there who prefer a burst of bygone times.

Smiths Salt 'n' Shake opened my eyes to the glory of crisps: the crunch, the hit of salt, those golden discs of potato filling my belly as I munched them while rolling along Harold Street on my roller skates. I learned the excitement of finding an extra-giant crisp, or one that looked like a face, or a cloud. And I learned the happiness of the last bits of the packet when you flatten the bag, tip your head back and swallow the crisp dust.

They were a gateway to other flavours, which made their appearance in my world in the eighties, when supermarket brands were taking off and the mighty multipack came into fashion. My Mam would bring home a couple of these multi-packs on Fridays – she'd scream at me and my brother David to help unload the car instead of simply standing by the boot eating cheese and onion crisps and giving each other dead arms. There were four regular flavours in the multipacks, and the packets had specific colours: green (cheese and onion), blue (salt and vinegar), red (ready salted) and brown (beef; this was only for the grown-ups). These packet colours are cemented into my heart, and when Walkers changed them in the nineties by switching round the cheese and onion and salt and vinegar, I saw the move as wanton anarchy – and I still do today. Onions are green, therefore cheese and onion should be green; salt is found in the sea, and the sea is blue, ergo salt and vinegar packets should be blue. The old system made sense! The word ready in 'ready salted' contains the word 'red', so it is imperative that they leave this packet red, or else society may well break down altogether.

Crisps really came into their own in the Dent house at Christmas. For us, Christmas was only really Christmas when at least two or three family-sized packs of crisps were squeezed into the gaps on top of the cupboards as they were too big to store anywhere else; this was the sign that the festive season was truly underway. Mam had done her big Christmas shop, and then the second one that was 'just for odds and sods', and then the third one that was completely unnecessary and simply for the excitement of a jam-packed Christmas supermarket and all the reduced-sticker bargains. For a lot of mams in the eighties – and I feel this now, too, of course – Christmas was not about baby Jesus or goodwill to all men, it was about the magic that could be gleaned in an NCP car park traffic jam at 4 p.m. on 22 December, bumper to bumper, defying the odds and making Christmas happen once again.

And yet despite the fridge groaning with reduced-price rum butter and cheese straws, it was imperative that the Dent kids did not begin eating the stuff too early. You couldn't just go in that fridge willy-nilly on the morning of the twentieth and begin merrily eating duck pâté on your toast. No, that was for Christmas Day teatime. How about cutting into a buttercream-covered Yule log? NO! That was for Boxing Day when Aunty Clare was coming over. It was agony. The one place Mam did turn a blind eye, though, was crisps.

'Put a few crisps in a bowl,' she'd say as we were settling down to watch one of the Christmas specials on telly. It might be *Family Fortunes* with Les Dennis, or Val Doonican's Christmas show, where he sang in that soothing voice of his while donning a variety of smart-casual jerseys. Now *that* was prime 'start the Christmas crisps' television. Maybe a bowl of prawn cocktail ones might start doing the rounds, or perhaps even some fancy barbecued beef crisps with their skins still on from Marks & Spencer. If we were pushing our luck, we might even convince Mam to bring out the fancy Christmas dip quartet, the ones that came in a plastic tray: there was a white yoghurty one, a white cheesy one, a tomatoey salsa-type one and some sort of guacamole that no one ever ate. Eating crisps with dips felt very sophisticated. It was like what posh people definitely did at their soirées over in Stanwix Bank, the posh part of Carlisle – not that we'd ever been invited to one.

Of course, I am remembering this family bonhomie with rose-tinted spectacles. In reality we probably bickered all the way through Van Doonican. 'He's so bloody boring!' fourteen-year-old me would say. 'Why are we watching a man in a cardigan sing "Little Drummer Boy" beside a fake coal fire? And why do all those backing singers keep pretending he's fit and laughing at his jokes? It's mekking me feel sick. And why can't I just go to the pub? All my friends are in the pub. Yes, all of them Mam, everyone is allowed to go but me!'

'Well at least I can hear every word Val Doonican is singing!' Mam would say while casually dipping a turkey and stuffing crisp into some substandard tzatziki. 'Not like those morons you listen to, mumbling through their mouths! They all mumble. And that Morrissey, falling about with a bloody bouquet of gladioli hanging out his arse pocket singing songs about getting hit by a bus . . . don't make me laugh! And you can go to the pub for all I care, off you go, but it will be the last thing you do in this house! Wait, can anyone smell burning? I think the dog has singed its tail again on the gas fire.'

And then my Dad would chime in: 'Is there any more of these prawn cocktail crisps? 'Ere, Grace, go and stick us a few in a bowl. And bring me a glass of hock. I've got it out the fridge so it's a bit warmer. I used to drink it when I was in Germany. Did I ever tell you about when I lived in Germany . . . ?'

'Can we open the Quality Street, Mam?' my brother David would ask. 'Can we open the tin? Come on, Mam, it's nearly Christmas. We'll just have one each and shut it again. Go on Mam, please . . .'

'No!' Mam would say. 'Cos then you'll all be looking at me on Christmas Day asking what I'm going to do to put a smile on your bloody faces and I'll say, well you ate all the food and opened the chocolates, so what do you want? 'Ere, have some more crisps. Grace, go and put some more crisps in a bowl for your Dad. And stick the kettle on as I'll have a tea. OK, fine, bring the mince pies for afters. And someone use up this guancamolley thing. It's starting to get a skin.'

And although this moment in time is gone, and my parents are gone, and the dog is gone, and the family house is sold, and I'm now a grown adult who can have crisps any time I choose, I get goosebumps just thinking about it. In fact, every time someone puts crisps in a bowl to be fancy, well, I think about all of it.

Aisling Bea's

Potato Waffles with Spaghetti Hoops

aka *Petits cercles de pâtes dans une sauce tomate sur gaufres de pommes de terre avec beurre irlandais*

Aisling Bea is an actor, writer and stand-up comedian. Oh, and she's a BAFTA winner. She's someone I can't help but admire. She's simply one of those tenacious, beautiful, effervescent creatures who light up a room when they enter; she peppers the air with her warm but forceful Kildare accent, cracking one-liners while also somehow coming out with things that are utterly profound. She is a woman who grew up with mostly women, and not just any old women but women who worked in horse-racing. She says she doesn't find that amazing given that she didn't know any better; everyone just wanted to be a jockey, or was a jockey, or owned a race horse, or worked at the National Stud.

Aisling is one of those people you'd want on your side in a civil disturbance, as not only would she know what to do, but she would also make sure everyone got fed in the process. Food and sustenance are very important to her. We talked about her obsession with getting a proper breakfast down her before long days of filming her TV show *This Way Up*, and about her love of playing *Ready Steady Cook* with items in her fridge: cauliflower, hummus, sausages – *let's get cooking!* We also talked about the 'something nice' tin that her mother and sisters had in the house growing up, where nice things, such as biscuits or sweets, were kept. Growing up, she thought every house had a 'something nice' tin, and it took moving away from home for her to realise that that wasn't a normal thing.

All families are different, with quirks and catchphrases and secret languages, things we think are just normal but are actually idiosyncratically ours. But for the remainder of my life, the thing I will remember about Aisling Bea is something very practical indeed. Did you know you can butter potato waffles? Did you know that when you retrieve those waffles from under the grill or from the toaster, you can slather a large amount of salted Kerrygold butter on them, and that it will melt gloriously, creating a sort of toasted, mashed-potato mega hash brown on growth steroids. Why did I not think about this before?!

THE RECIPE

Box of potato waffles

Tin of spaghetti in tomato sauce; hoops are preferable

Block of Irish salted butter, Kerrygold if available as
    that's Aisling Bea's preferred choice; keep it at
    room temperature so you can spread it

Enter house. Pick up letter from gas supplier with generous news that they are freezing your tariff at a cost that will only require one kidney to be sold on the dark web.

Sigh loudly. Lament how it is only Tuesday when the week feels like it's been dragging on for nine and a half days.

Suspect you may be hangry. Place gas letter behind your copy of *The Big Fat Duck Cookbook* that you keep in the kitchen for dinner inspiration.

Stare into fridge. Behold the antique green pepper and the Philadelphia spread you are too scared to open in case it has become sentient.

Open freezer drawers and find delicious, welcoming box of potato waffles, smiling at you like loyal friends. Potato waffles are more reliable than your actual friends. Potato waffles have never borrowed £100 off you, then avoided you and posted a picture of themselves in Marbella a few weeks later.

Turn on grill. Retrieve two potato waffles from box. Tell yourself that 'this should be enough'. Laugh and remove another four potato waffles from box. (As if you couldn't eat ten in one sitting. This isn't your first rodeo.)

Feel pilot light of happiness flickering to life again. Place waffles into toaster. Think about the long arid years in the culinary Gobi Desert when you used to make these under the grill. Remember how amazed friends and acquaintances are when you tell them down the pub that you can cook waffles in a toaster.

Try to remember whether the dial that says '1–9' on the side of the toaster is for the number of minutes that food should take or the shade that toast should be. Wonder how this translates to waffles. Get a headache. Turn the dial up to 9; this recipe needs HEAT.

Remind yourself that whatever happens, you *must* turn the toaster down to 2 or you will overdo your toast later this week and set off the fire alarm. Again.

Forget this immediately.

Plunge the waffles down. Search for tin opener for the spaghetti hoops.

Look in the drawer. Look in the dishwasher. Look back in the drawer. Look in the sink. Look back in the drawer again. See chopsticks you stole from Itsu, and plastic sporks you saved as they'd be useful 'when you went camping'. Sigh loudly.

Realise the tin opener could have been packed in a random place by a child or a partner or guest who washed up. The enormity of this mystery is suddenly huge. If you have a teenager, the tin opener could even have left the building and be in the GCSE art block by now.

Say loudly, to anyone close by: 'Has anyone moved the tin opener?' Be aware that this is an open-ended question because everyone at some juncture in their household life has moved that tin opener, and the response may well be, 'You used it last, it's where you left it,' which will send you over the edge.

Become distracted by smell of waffles cooking. Smell air desperately, trying to gauge when the surface of the waffles is changing state from moist pallid mush to golden-brown deliciousness.

Hover over toaster trying to see the state of play. All you have is a warm nose and a view of the edges of the waffles least exposed to the heat. This is the worst of all scenarios.

Consider pressing emergency stop button on the side of the toaster, which will eject the waffles. It must be time by now. You can't risk burning them. They must be burning by now. You can smell burning!

Press eject. Realise waffles are thoroughly uncooked and were only in for forty-six seconds. What a journey you've been on. Make a mental note to remember this story for your biographer, or to tell on *Sunday Brunch* with Lovejoy and Rimmer.

Repeat this stage three times over the next three minutes.

Find tin opener. It was in the drawer down the side of the cutlery tray, laughing at you the whole time.

Realise spaghetti hoops tin has a ring-pull top. Whistle 'Life' by Des'Ree. Open tin and eat one cheeky spoonful.

Pour hoops into small bowl and place in microwave, ignoring the fact that the large glass plate has not been cleaned for days.

Overlook the other thirty-seven buttons on your state-of-the-art microwave and press HIGH > 3 MINUTES > START.

Stand by microwave scraping last remnants out of spaghetti hoops tin with a spoon.

Feel like your life is coming together again. Realise you are absolutely, completely ravenous and could literally eat this whole dinner standing up by the sink.

Lift waffles out of the toaster with your fingers making a sound like this: 'Aah, aaah, aah, bloody hell!' It's important the waffles are this hot for the next stage.

Take Irish butter and spread it liberally all over waffles. Use far more than decency allows. Smile beatifically as butter begins to settle in glistening pools.

Remove spaghetti hoops from microwave and spoon some over one of the waffles. Place another waffle on top of this first waffle. Add another layer of spaghetti hoops. Begin to create a spaghetti–waffle Leaning Tower of Pisa, with butter majestically seeping from its potato windows and staircases.

Take plate to lounge. Eat on your knees while watching a TV show called something like *Police! Lights! Action!* or *Britain's Worst Laybys*, or something where Michael Portillo goes to Saskatoon by train while wearing orange trousers.

Demolish entire serving, feeling resolutely better about the world.

SWEET TREATS

. . . And Why They Can Feel Like Therapy

When a dessert menu is moving about the table while I'm at a restaurant with friends, I'll often say, with a smugness that'll piss off everyone, 'Well, the thing is, I don't really have a sweet tooth . . .' This is something I firmly believe about myself. It's something that I would use at the gates of heaven as a bargaining tool for the sins of lust, greed and envy, all of which I have been very guilty of.

What I actually mean when I say this is that I don't have a sweet tooth like my parents or Gran did. All three of them were absolute fiends for sugary items and anything sponge-based, particularly when those things were made with whipped cream or jam, or wrapped in bright sparkly foils. I was brought up by humans who had lived through an era with a real scarcity of sweetness. They reminisced about living on things like unsweetened porridge oats, and my Gran in particular recalled times when the whole street would pool their sugar-rationing coupons to make a single wedding cake. They existed in a world where seeing an actual piece of fruit was exciting, and they'd tell me about the day Tilbury Road got its first banana as if it was yesterday. More importantly, though, they remembered the excitement post war when sugar came into their lives in full force, when the cake shop shelves began to fill up again, and when tubs of Quality Street began appearing at Christmas. I feel this moulded many of our attitudes to sweetness for life.

When sugar was around, I saw my often anxious parents, with their very adult worries about money and life, suddenly become giddily happy – and that in turn made me happy, too. The Dents were happy at the country pub at Sunday lunch when the creaky sweet trolley had a big wobbly trifle with layers of Swiss roll slices and custard. We were extra happy on holidays in Blackpool where the hotel buffet had unlimited iced fairy cakes, chocolate frosted buttercreams and glamorous crèmes brûlées as the final stage of dinner, setting us up to go enjoy the cabaret. The Dents were thrilled in the eighties when enormous supermarkets began being built on the edge of town, the ones that would sell ten doughnuts for a pound and mark down fresh cream choux buns to mere pennies at closing. And we were overjoyed when a place called the Toby Carvery opened in Carlisle, offering among other things a dessert menu of classic British puddings: spotted dick, jam roly-poly and other jingoistic foods designed to cheer up a small damp island. Everything was served with custard in an 'everlasting' style, which meant that for a fixed price they would refill your custard jug to infinity and never, ever stop.

My Gran's house felt like Hansel and Gretel's house. The woman may not have had any fondness for children, reserving her greatest affection for Jack Russells, but the place still swam in sugary things that gave any guest a warm welcome. Fox's Glacier Mints and boxes of chocolate-covered hazelnuts sat on the sideboard to munch through on Sundays when we were allowed to sit in the 'good room' at the front of the house and listen to Jim Reeves LPs, washing it down with glasses of Barr's dandelion and burdock, cola or cream soda. In her kitchen, a five-tier cake tin was always chock full of KitKats, Breakaways, Club bars and freshly made rock buns; tier five always had some sort of iced cake that she'd bought from the local Women's Institute cake stand. It was never kisses from Gran, nor cuddles, but you knew you were in her good books when she said: 'Go and git yoursel' a biscuit frae the tin . . . git yerself two if you want.'

I didn't just see sugar make the adults happy, though. I saw it make them greedy. I saw them hoard it and hide it, and this just made it more exciting. A general rule of thumb in the Dent house was that the more delicious a sweet thing was, the more difficult it was to reach. For example: my Mam's favourite mint Viscount biscuits were stored in the spare bedroom on top of the wardrobe, only reachable if you stood on the handles of her exercise bike and hooked the packet towards you with the boomerang that Aunt Elsie brought back from Albury–Wodonga. I was specifically told not to eat these biscuits, and yet those mint Viscounts, wrapped in slightly bitter dark chocolate with their creamy hit of pale green peppermint oil, tasted all the more special for being forbidden.

This feeling of mischief and joy when it comes to sweet treats has stayed with me ever since. It comes out each time I see a tray of brightly wrapped biscuits left on a table in a boring meeting room, or when I go to a restaurant and see the words 'banana split' or 'knickerbocker glory' written on a menu. I watch it play out time and again when I sit with the great and good of the jaded food world, who eat for a living but still dissolve into glee when a chef says 'banoffee', 'raspberry ripple' or 'buttery biscuit base'.

For the Dents, sugar was our hobby, our pastime, our therapy. We had Peek Freans Chocolate Assortment tins in my family, not Prozac; we had custard creams, not counselling. It felt like there was no deep-rooted generational trauma that could not be ignored by eating a bowl of syrup-laden peaches topped with delicious Tip Top cream.

I know some of you probably feel sick after reading all that. I'll admit it: perhaps I do have a sweet tooth after all. These days, when I'm recording the podcast, nothing gets hoovered up more quickly after the guests have gone than the leftover sugary snacks. The remnants of the Dairy Milk that Siobhán McSweeney brought along to eat with Guinness? Disappeared down my throat in several short bursts as we were packing up the microphones. (More on that later.) How about Krishnan Guru-Murthy's rice pudding and raspberry jam? We bought three cans for the recording: one for him, one for me and one spare for a photo. I ate the third for dinner with a double-big blob of Bonne Maman jam; I'd been feeling far too pooped to cook, and now I had this delicious, calming, balm-like rice in its pretty blue tin that reminded me of begging Mam for pudding after tea (after some sheer nonsense-talk about how we should really be eating more fruit, she would relent). We recorded Craig David's Christmas special on the coldest wintry day and he requested Ben & Jerry's cookie dough ice cream. I do not even like Ben & Jerry's, and yet over the course of that next week a hungry ghost made the ice cream disappear from the freezer. Spooky.

For many of us, sugar is tied intimately to some of our fondest memories as children, and these memories are full of fun, happiness and joy, of being cared for and looked after and not having to worry about a thing in the 'real' world – as adults we crave that as much as we crave sugar. Above all, what sweet treats have to offer us is comfort. That's why they're still a part of my life, despite my knowing that they aren't exactly the healthiest thing in the world.

—

Still, despite sweet, brightly coloured things in shiny wrappers absolutely sparking joy, I think it's the most bland, boring, beige things that sometimes do the most for us, at least in the UK. Whenever we check into a chain hotel feeling tired and we see that the cleaner has left a dual packet of complimentary short-bread cookies inside a coffee cup beside the sachets of UHT milk and some ground coffee that tastes like gravel, well, it's enough to make us cry. I have lost count of the number of times when I have fallen into bed clutching those little tartan packets, the ones that often come with a picture of a Highland cow on them despite the fact the biscuits are made in Slough. I'm always quietly thankful hotels limit their output to two biscuits a stay. If they left an entire packet of Jammie Dodgers, I would consume the whole lot.

And it's not even just the Brits that think this. When the musical legend Rufus Wainwright came on, he brought what he rather adorably called 'digestible biscuits' – aka a packet of McVitie's digestives. I was touched that even a Canadian could love the healing power of the bland, beige British biscuit. Rufus grew up with Anglophile tastes as his father, the singer Loudon Wainwright, lived in Hampstead, and so he spent long summer holidays in London. His fondness for digestives specifically came from a time when his mother lived with an English boyfriend who would serve them smeared with whiffy blue cheese. For Rufus, these digestives were the epitome of low-key Britishness and cosiness. How we love sludge-coloured things masquerading as treats.

My own love of bland sweetness dates right back to my time

with Farley's rusks, in the first three years of my life. They were my very first exposure to sweet things making everything better. Back then, boxes of Farley's rusks came with two serving suggestions: either dry and as they came, bigger than a baby's head, or mushed up in milk in a bowl, looking like porridge but tasting like the yummy milk that goes around cereal (or, more accurately, tasting like love and a simpler time where my diary held almost nothing between 7 a.m. and 1 p.m., after which I'd promptly be put down for my nap – bliss). There was actually a middle ground between these 'dry' and 'wet' options, though, which was when the rusk was still intact but soggy and on the cusp of falling apart, having been clutched and sucked upon for hours.

Farley's rusks were (and still are) the ultimate toddler distracter, a moveable feast to go away and busy themselves with when Mummy was too worn out and tired. Whenever Mam was trying to chuck Ajax powder at loo rims or warm up marrowfat peas in a pan, they'd be on hand. They were there to soothe me, to shut me up as I sat by the TV in my poncho covered in crumbs, mashing the remainder of the last rusk into the chassis of my little red toy car before crying upon realising there was none left.

'Why are you crying, would you like another rusk?' my Mam would say, giving me another fragrant portion for me to smush among Stickle Bricks or into corners of the Fisher Price Activity Centre. It was sublime, that fresh rusk taken from the rustling packet and handed to me while Mam sat juggling my little baby brother David on her knee, probably wondering if it was really such a good idea to have another baby so soon. I ate rusks and other sweet things to iron out the tension at home, before I was even old enough to know what tension was.

I'm thoroughly unsurprised that many of us can't and won't ever let sugar go. Farley's rusks remain one of my most embarrassing comfort eating crutches. I have hidden this admission here, in the very last chapter: to this day I carry around a packet of Farley's rusks wherever I go. I usually pick mine up in Boots. I'll be loading my trolley with all the lacquers and varnishes and cotton pads and chemical removal liquids that make me the natural beauty I am, and then right at the end pop in a box of rusks and eat one surreptitiously on the 97 bus home. The boxes now come with a disclaimer that proclaims they have no added sugar, almost as if they're aware of their own sweet, addictive past, as if they know about the sugary crumbs I had in my cot and in my shoes back then. They are far less sweet now, yes, but they are just as comfortingly delicious, and even though I am a very big girl, crumbs find their way into the lining of my handbag, crumbs that taste of Mam and love.

There is another emotion present when we choose sweet and sugary: the exquisite joy of free will. Sweet things are, for most of us, our very first taste of choosing for ourselves. Many of us were taken into shops as tiny tots and allowed to point at things and make a decision all on our own. Freddo Frogs or Milky Way Stars? It's up to you, you choose! The sense of agency is exhilarating and unforgettable.

If you stuck your hand right down the side of our sofa in the seventies and eighties, you could sometimes find the money to fund a trip to the shops. God bless couch treasure, the spare coins that had fallen from Dad's pockets and become tangled in Quality Street wrappers from last Christmas, caught between our cat Sooty's missing collar and numerous Coral betting-shop pens. There was a chance you might put your hand down too far and cut your finger on a rough tack, but the risk was worth it for the opportunity to explore the outer limits of your imagination, be it lemon drops, cola cubes or those packets of chocolate cigarettes that we'd use to mimic our parents smoking their Embassy Number Ones. The corporate world spends millions of pounds per year on 'team-building' days to 'break the ice' between colleagues. In reality, all you need to do is stick people in a room and ask them what they chose at the sweet shop when they were younger. People's stiffness would simply dissolve and you would find complete strangers discussing the merits of a yellow sherbet Dip Dab over crackling Space Dust with huge enthusiasm. These are vital matters, and everyone has an opinion on them.

It took scrutiny and deliberation on those first solo trips to my local newsagents in Currock to buy sweeties. At five years old, all three and a half feet of me figured out what was what pretty quickly: I had a particular fondness for the pint-pot sweets that tasted oddly of beer, and when my friends and I bought them we'd sway around pretending to be drunk; I realised that I hated liquorice Black Jacks, the ones wrapped in waxy paper, instead preferring the large oblong-shaped Refresher sweets that came in bright blue paper with orange writing; I didn't care for Parma Violets and would much rather have yellow flumpy bananas; and I knew lollypops left me emotionally cold, just like those gobstoppers that all the lads along our street ate to look macho, preferring to hunt down milk-flavoured teeth.

With our selection of sweets finalised in our little sweaty hands, we approached the newsagent. We were kids making our first ever purchases, not quite able to see over the counter, let alone to know the proper etiquette of shops. We would loiter for hours, asking the price of every penny sweet a dozen times, because occasionally – very, very occasionally – some of the larger sweets were twopence, and with our limited sense of arithmetic this was very scary. What if we spent too much? The police would come and put us in jail! Somehow we would avoid the slammer and head back up the lane with our bags of sweet things, chomping and laughing. We were hooked on these moments for ever.

It wasn't long after those first trips to the newsagents that my Dad and me would start taking walks to the minimart when we needed to do a speedy shopping run. I'd be skipping over puddles, dancing and yelling and shouting after him to look at whatever nonsense I was doing the entire way there, and when we were about fifty yards away he'd pick me up and plop me on his hip, whisking me to the entrance. He'd run around the shop, grabbing things like loo roll and bin bags 'for Mam' as if these were special gifts that only she would appreciate, and I'd be laughing the entire time. The best part of this jaunt would be the paying up part, when we'd get to the shelves near the till filled with Fry's Turkish Delight, Topics and Golden Cups. These things, he told me, were for 'big girls', not small ones like me, and small girls couldn't have big girls' chocolate, but if I begged and begged and begged I knew I could get him to buy me some Cadbury Buttons. After he gave in, he'd tell me that if we hurried, we would get back in time for the cartoons, and we'd run all the way home and cuddle up on the sofa in front of the telly, sharing the chocolate.

We used to do this in the later years of my Dad's life, too, in the gap after dementia took his ability to drive but before it took his compulsion to roam, when we'd walk to the Morrisons supermarket that was half a mile from his retirement flat. This was the flat where he watched *Fawlty Towers* on his sixty-five-inch telly, making his way through a box of scones with jam and cream while simultaneously moaning that his late-onset diabetes was playing up. Towards the end of his life, everything in that flat needed to be boxed up and taken away; me and my brother spent many drab hours loading ceramic knick-knacks, horse brass and cruise-ship memorabilia into boxes, lingering over a framed, autographed poster of James 'Sugar Spun' Martin, who Mam and Dad met when he cooked on a cruise ship. When I began working in the same industry as him, Mam always secretly hoped that he and I would fall in love and get married. I'd be set for fancy puddings for life! How could anyone be happier than that?

We did those walks to the supermarket on most days, and they took a lot longer than they used to. They started to take up more and more of my days, and soon enough they took up the entirety of my days, days when I really needed to be somewhere else three hundred miles away but just couldn't bring myself to leave. We'd walk slowly, mere steps in an hour, examining the hedgerows, spotting the occasional squirrel, taking in the fresh air. I'd listen to his stories as we crept along and would get a little confused myself. Some of them might have been true and some of them might have been pure confabulation. Dementia makes time like a squeezebox, opening and closing the gaps between eras. Was this the eighties or the nineties he was talking about?

We'd be in and out of the Morrisons with the same two things every time: a bag of Cadbury Buttons and a newspaper. He couldn't even read any more, but he had me get it just to go through the motions.

'Hurry up Dad, we'll get back for that last bit of *Murder She Wrote*!' I'd say on the way back, opening up the bag of Cadbury Buttons. One for him, one for me, one for him, one for me. 'Do you remember buying me these, Dad, when I was a little girl?' He nodded yes, but I could tell he couldn't really remember. The buttons still taste the same as they did back then, and the packet is still the same shade of purple.

Cadbury wrappers will always signify love for me. Cadbury was the missing link between me and Dad, bridging the gap that plain words could not. I loved Dad, of course, but he died leaving more questions than answers about his personal life, about who he actually was, about how many children he actually had, about the various black holes regarding his whereabouts over the years. I am on much safer ground, emotionally, when I think of the things I know for certain. I know we both loved Cadbury Fudge Fingers, that sweet slab of soft, yielding, sticky fudge wrapped in milk chocolate, and how we loved to sing along with the 'Finger of Fudge' advert any time it was on TV; the ad was set to a descant recorder backing track, and it had small boys running out of a dusty school looking all glum, only for joy to be brought to their faces upon being given a Fudge Finger. We also shared great affection for the Cadbury Curly Wurly, a weird, chewy tree trunk of caramel with a chocolate glaze which my Dad blamed fully for pulling out one of his wisdom teeth.

At Christmas we'd go to Woolworths together to choose presents, both of us equally fascinated by the huge pile of Cadbury selection boxes where you'd get all the big hitters together: a Wispa, a Flake, a Crunchie and a Dairy Milk! Dad would buy me and David a selection box and then inevitably eat the whole thing while watching TV in mid-December. I didn't begrudge him anything, as I loved him. Mam would make him buy another one for us, and we'd sit down watching the telly again, Dad making up silly words to the adverts and eating my chocolates, because he was very silly.

People tell me Cadbury chocolate is cheap and nasty. They tell me that I can buy Montezuma's 74 per cent dark chocolate buttons at about £4 a bag. But fancy chocolate buttons do not evoke autumn leaves, damp socks and the smell of my father's Brut 33 face-splash. They are not his bristles whisking my cheek as I cling to him as we walk past the frozen peas and the greeting cards. They are not the essence of being up past bedtime watching *Police 5* with Shaw Taylor: 'Keep 'em peeled,' the presenter would say, asking us to be vigilant of villains who had stolen bikes and pilfered antiques from garden centres.

I'm not really sure where the time goes. Now it's Christmas 2022, and me, my brother and my sister-in-law Tam are sitting vigil with my dying Dad. I've been there for so many December days, looking for signs he's gone, putting my fingers to his neck to check, and then carrying on reading him bits from the Cumberland newspapers. But despite my constant watch, he's gone quietly, without me noticing. He's lying there, still and peaceful. 'Happy Xmas (War Is Over)' is playing on Radio Carlisle, and as I look at him I'm mesmerised by how, as the skin around his face retracts, he resembles me more closely than I have ever known. Our wonky teeth, our jutting jaws, our strange ear lobes.

After the paperwork has been signed, when everything's official, the three of us gather up the last of his things. In his bedside drawer there's a Cadbury Dairy Milk bar; we take it, divvy it up and eat it in silence. I keep the wrapper. The purple of that wrapper will always be my tiny hand wrapped around Dad's finger. Always.

Siobhán McSweeney's

Dairy Milk, Tayto and Guinness

It is impossible not to love the TV comedy *Derry Girls*. The writing is machine-gun sharp, and the cast are so believable as awful but endearing nineties schoolgirls, coping with hormones, mothers and the daily trudge of life at Our Lady Immaculate College in Derry. Funnily enough though, the breakout star of the show was not one of the 'girls' themselves but Siobhán McSweeney, who won a BAFTA for playing Sister Michael: nun, headmistress and wonderfully deadpan sociopath.

Sister Michael – via Lisa McGee's incredible writing – appeared to be someone who had clearly sinned greatly in her previous life and was now being punished through the medium of school trips to Paris, woefully long assemblies, awful talent shows and having to ward off the local boys' school students hoping to snog her teenage charges. She sighed through each and every moment, and I loved her all the more for it. There is, I feel, a little Sister Michael in all of us.

Siobhán arrived at my house in the summer of 2021. This was about four months after my mother had died and I was beginning to wear a semblance of normality on my face, getting through (almost) entire days without thinking about it. Having one of my favourite actresses over to chat was pretty good as far as distractions go, to be fair, though I just wished it wasn't on a day that was so hot that the backs of my knees were dripping. It was one of those days when I realised at some point I would need to accept that the valley between my boobs would simply need to be mopped. Believe me when I say that there is no glamorous way to do this, but Siobhán understood.

Siobhán is, like all the best actresses, magnetic to be around, sweeping from Brechtian profundity to surreal silliness in seconds. She is relentlessly honest and bullshit-free, someone who I feel would be the friend you called before doing something daft because you know she'd give you both barrels of honesty, before and afterwards.

What I loved about the snack she brought along was that it was three items eaten at the same time, in the same mouth, to create a whole mood board of emotions: a slab of Dairy Milk, a packet of Tayto cheese and onion crisps and a can of Guinness. I stopped drinking alcohol towards the end of that summer, and I am oddly pleased to think that one of the last alcoholic drinks that passed my lips was a can of Guinness with Siobhán McSweeney. We shoved a large chunk of chocolate in our mouths, chewed until it became sticky, and shoved in two or three crisps before continuing to chew, washing the whole thing down with a swig of Guinness.

'There,' she said. 'There it is!'

I didn't quite understand what she meant. I struggled with the sensation of eating something that was salty, cheesy, boozy and chocolatey all at the same time. The sweetness was enhancing the saltiness, and the chocolate shouldn't go with the cheese, yet it sort of somehow does. My brain just wouldn't let me compute it, and at one point I was worried that this whole mess might threaten to come back up again.

'That's it, that's the taste,' she said. 'That's being in the pub with my dad as a little girl, and him buying me crisps and chocolate and letting me have the froth off his pint. It is magical.'

And there it is. There is no purer explanation of the podcast than that. It's about those flavours and smells that combine to drag you back to a time when the people you loved were still around, when things felt most simple. And if other people think that thing is disgusting, well, frankly, that's their business.

THE RECIPE

1 large bar Dairy Milk chocolate (850 grams should do)
1 packet Tayto cheese and onion crisps (or two or three,
    depending on how you're feeling)
1 can Guinness

Source unnecessarily large bar of Dairy Milk chocolate. Your best bet is any W. H. Smith shop, where it will be pushed upon you if you buy a copy of Richard Osman's latest novel. Sigh and accept that you will now consume almost all of it on a short train ride home.

Purchase some bags of Tayto cheese and onion crisps by simply going to the local shop in Derry, or any part of Northern Ireland or the Republic of Ireland, where they are sold in abundance. Easy.

Hang on. You're not in Northern Ireland or the Republic of Ireland? Do not panic. Simply find somebody who lives in these places, telephone them and explain that you do not have access to Tayto crisps. Tell them you are on the brink of Walkers instead, which you 'guess will be just as good. I mean, what's the difference?' Hang up phone and wait by the letterbox: a large package of Tayto crisps will arrive within two to three working days.

Place cans of Guinness in fridge, beside decaying lettuce and a jar of 'sticky toffee pudding body paint' that someone bought you for Christmas. Make an intention to sort your life out soon, just not today.

Prepare cosy nest on sofa: take off occasional cushions,

knitted throw, sofa duvet, magazines, university projects, remote controls, laptop chargers, cats, cat toys, discarded bras and biscuit wrappers. Sweep away cat hair and crumbs. Replace cushions, throw and duvet and behold your new home for the day.

Turn on TV and find a show about something like people in America who are untenably sad about their personal existences due to divorce or fatal illness, until a man called Hank with a tool belt shows them how much nicer life is with Onyx kitchen countertops. (NB: Do not attempt to watch anything involving news or current affairs, and avoid anything with David Attenborough narrating the painful inevitable cruelty of the natural world where a baby elephant gets lost from its mummy in a sandstorm. No. If in any doubt, put on ITV2 and choose any entertainment vehicle involving Natasha from Atomic Kitten.)

Bring cold Guinness, slab of Dairy Milk and Tayto crisps to the sofa. Rest packet of crisps on your belly. Open can of Guinness; decant Guinness into a glass, if there's a clean one. Open chocolate, inhaling the glorious Dairy Milk aroma.

Snap off five or six chunks of Dairy Milk and post them directly into your mouth, just to check if this is indeed the exact same Dairy Milk taste you have been eating all of your life. Despite being fully aware that there are better chocolates in the world, remind yourself that you would be prepared to die in a duel to defend Dairy Milk's honour.

Sip Guinness. Yes, it does taste a bit like muddy iron. That's the point. No, it's not half as nice as banana Nesquik or a Costa Coffee tropical mango bubble frappé, but that also isn't the point. Guinness is meant to be difficult; the more you drink, the more sense it makes.

Open crisps. If you are a Tayto-eating newbie, grudgingly accept that these crisps are absolutely freaking delicious, delivering a far stronger hit of cheese than others; consider giving up life as you know it and moving to Kilkenny to get a daily fix.

The moment has arrived. Place large chunk of Dairy Milk into your mouth, followed by several large crisps. Chew loudly and, as you are alone, with your mouth slightly open like a cement mixer. Pour Guinness into mouth, experiencing the full range of human emotion.

Swallow while flicking channel to TLC, where a woman is attempting to pay for her dream wedding by bulk-buying boxes of pumpkin spice Cheerios.

Repeat.

Dent's Dictionary Corner

A Series of Comfort Eating Things That Don't Have an Official Name But Really Should

Ambrosingly: the quiet admiration felt specifically on reading that Vanessa Feltz was drinking custard, again.

Beveragewiddling: guiltily sipping a cup of tea while on the toilet, imagining that nobody else anywhere in the history of planet Earth has ever had the idea to do something so thoroughly grotty.

Bossop's Blip: the precise moment you realise coming to do the big shop while hungry was a terrible, terrible error as your trolley is 90 per cent Ice Magic and Spooky Salt and Vinegar Starships.

Brink's Mat Biscuits: a repurposed shortbread tin masquerading as a sewing-supplies box; often tucked underneath a pile of clothes in a back room, and where you are currently hiding KitKats from your own children.

Bundleslodge: an inexplicable sadness at the decline of modern civilisation upon noticing that Wall's Mint Viennetta no longer has the same intricate multi-layered chocolate architecture it did in the eighties.

Calabassing: imagining this is how Kim Kardashian lives as you buy the expensive hummus with a slick of oil on it.

Celebrhateration: feeling weirdly defensive on hearing one's favourite Celebration chocolate being slagged off – how dare these people, your friends for decades, slag off the humble Bounty?

Clottedcremumbrage: a previously amiable chat about the order of jam and cream on scones that has tipped viciously into Cornish devolution and a time someone called Jethro sprayed some campers in Redruth with slurry.

Coddleswagget: a minor but meaningful act of self-love experienced in Maccy D's ordering the Filet-o-Fish, blasé about the fact that it takes six minutes extra because it will be freshly made and hot – babes, you are worth it.

Colonel Marvin's Platoon: a fictional marching army for whom you appear to have measured out pasta despite only cooking for two persons.

Coolblueyawn: the unappreciated skill of opening your face as wide as a Brabantia 120-litre bin in order to swallow a cloud of Dorito dust that is only accessible from the crevices of a grab bag via some deft origami.

CrumbleCrimeScene: a ten-square-metre area between the kitchen and the sofa strewn with discarded socks and toast crusts, leading to a puddle by a freezer door that gives you all the circumstantial evidence required to pin down a teenager's whereabouts between 11 p.m. and 1 a.m.

Cumblesberry Corner: a small cluster of former party animals, ex-cocaine users and sex addicts huddled together at a house party intensely discussing air fryers.

DairyQuadbangle: a lively altercation in a public house over your conviction that Easter egg chocolate tastes better than everyday chocolate.

E-numberescobarring: sneaking your own strawberry laces and sherbet flying saucers into a Vue cinema and eating them in the dark, feeling like a narco-terrorist.

Extra-Sized Dunkleglomp: a thirty-centimetre-diameter salted caramel white chocolate chip cookie, bigger than your own head, which is only available from a kiosk on a British mainline-station railway concourse.

Favamoongeyepeas: a can of mysterious pulses, with a label in a foreign language, that you're not adventurous enough to use in a recipe in place of chickpeas, so they live in your store cupboard for twenty-two years.

Fishlewhiff: a perilous seventy-seven-second window of stirring canned tuna into a warm pasta sauce as it goes from the pits of stinking hell to completely delicious.

Flumpyfossoping: the wanton exuberance of starting a Thorntons Continental Selection without even glancing at the box.

Fnarrtington-Beresford: the childish urge that arises every November to have the word 'BUMSEX' laser-imprinted on top of the Quality Street tin while in John Lewis.

Frappalappacuddle: when globalism sucks but the server getting your name right in Starbucks as they passed you your caramel Frappuccino was the most tender part of a horrible day.

Fromagesnickle: a confused chat about whether cheese gets better or worse the mouldier it becomes, the answer to which is revealed forty-eight hours later with a short hospitalisation.

Fromagewangling: scraping a block of red Leicester with a knife and then pouring the fistful of crumbs directly into your mouth so as to fool your body into thinking it is not actually consuming calories.

Fuckoffaccia: a loaf of artisan Italian sourdough loaded with whole fresh Nocellara olives stored near the door of a hipster bakery that you will soon have no recollection of paying ten pounds for.

Goodbyesconeslope: a patch in almost every adult human's mid-thirties to mid-forties life when all leisure time is spent eating scones in a garden centre listening to their parents talk about wheelie bins, red squirrels and hospital appointments. Treasure it.

Greapling: the fake smile you do at a stranger's extremely precise, slightly passive-aggressive tea order, as they describe the closest Dulux paint shade to their requirements and the precise length of the milk splosh.

Gromblesnott: the abject hell of someone quietly adding 'And we can all share anyway' mere seconds after everyone in a group has thoughtfully placed their own highly personal Chinese takeaway order.

Himblegasm: the seven seconds of heart-breaking optimism between saving the second half of the double Milky Way

for tomorrow, neatly folding the packet, and scoffing
the lot.

Jambleswag: a collection of miniature 'Sweet Tip' raspberry
conserves stolen over the years from boutique hotel
breakfast buffets which you don't want but can't bring
yourself to throw away. You are now doomed to cart these
with you in various house moves until death.

Jingleglossop: An effusively written inter-faith holiday greeting
card delivered in December, from a bloke called Sarvesh
because your mid-week purchases of dal makhani have
recently bought him a lovely second-hand Renault Captur.

Jocasta's Joy Bar: a gluten-free, organic, handmade, small-
batch cocoa-nib protein bar – usually containing more fat
and refined carbs than a king-size Snickers – bought in a
Holland & Barrett after ashtanga yoga to null the pain of
farting during a downward dog.

Libbymippering: that moment halfway through singing the
amazing 1980s Um Bongo advert when you realise it's
probably quite reductive about the daily life of people in the
Democratic Republic of the Congo.

Littlelolorossoism: sheepishly adding a large dollop of garlic
and chive Philadelphia to every pasta dish when no one is
looking, passing it off as if you're Stanley Tucci.

MacPope: the quasi-holy presence in your friendship group
or family who collects everyone's Big Mac gherkins during
a McDonald's trip and eats them like communion wafers.
Blessed be the pickle eaters.

Meowsterchef: sharing a tin of tuna with your own cat, but putting salad cream in yours because you have a fractionally more sophisticated palate.

No-El's Given: eating a forgotten, dusty chocolate tree decoration found in the loft in early December while retrieving the Christmas tree; may be a tad mouldy. Still delicious.

Nibwaffling: the long, shame-sodden preamble about cocoa quality and favourite luxury chocolate brands which all middle-class people must offer before accepting and really enjoying a Freddo Frog.

Oatyglumping: buying 250 tubs of Pret a Manger porridge at £3.95 a go over a financial year rather than keeping one large bag of Costco microwave oats at work, because you just can't face Mable from Finance in the shared kitchen updating you on her dog Muffin's congested bum glands.

Oblique Coronary Snuffledom: The warm joy of one whole hour to yourself in a Costa Coffee between meetings, with a giant chocolate marshmallow teacake and 537 missed messages on your favourite WhatsApp group chat.

Oxenholmishing: the mysterious and never disclosed reason an Avanti Pendolino train has to close the on-board shop between Lancaster and Preston for 'stock-keeping' when it has only been open ninety minutes and only sells KitKats and plastic cups of scalding PG Tips.

PapaJohnuflexing: a quiet moment of contemplation for the genius who placed the pepperoni inside the stuffed crust.

Pharoah's Revenge: the woe of freezer bread that you wedged into the drawer too hastily; it is now hieroglyph-shaped and too crumpled to fit into the toaster.

Philoakeyness: the sheepish, blissful high of a Friday night 'catch-up' dinner with people you love being cancelled . . . allowing you to watch *Top of the Pops 1983* while eating tablespoons of Primula squirty cheese.

Pippinmas: an arduous two-week calendar window where staff agree to swap birthday cakes for fruit baskets until a stockpile of underripe guavas has Colin the Caterpillar rearing his delicious face again.

Porquelinology: not knowing a single thing about your own family genealogy but being heavily invested in Percy and Penny Pig's extended family tree.

Rick Moranis Syndrome: The wild anarchy of using self-raising flour for a recipe that specifically requires plain . . . followed by the creeping terror that your baking will quadruple in size, destroying the kitchen and ultimately your life.

Sauce of Resentment: a twenty-year war of attrition with a life partner over whether tomato ketchup lives in the fridge or the cupboard.

Rowntreesed: the reassurance of seeing a Lion bar in a bodega in a faraway country and knowing that if you wanted you could buy one and be home within a bite.

Scimplesuck: the heady thrill, just before successfully sucking a raspberry pip out of your own teeth, of whether the sheer force of sucking might vacuum out a chunk of your own brain, or at the very least a kidney.

Slombleflasser: someone watching Netflix while dining on a jar of silverskin pickles with their bare hands, making loud comments about the Michelin-starred maestro's 'lack of vision'.

Slopplegrimp: the quiet terror that sets in on wondering what the grey sludge inside the delicious plump pouches of supermarket tinned ravioli actually consists of.

Snafflemyersing: buying Halloween Haribo and Mr Kipling's Fiendish Fancies for the street's trick-or-treat evening as you're an upstanding citizen, only to switch off all the lights at 6 p.m. on 31 October and lie on the floor eating them.

Snottlegribbling: mindlessly eating chocolate rice crispy cakes from a primary school cake bake, even though you know they probably contain bogies, and not even your own child's bogies.

Spikeysmuggage: a warm, uncharitable inner glow that sets in after a neighbour's party when your cheddar and pineapple porcupine got more attention, love and respect than the hosts' new eighty-five-thousand-quid mock-Venetian patio.

Strumplegrunt: the horror on a control freak's face when someone opens the dishwasher door midway through a four-and-a-half-hour eco cycle to grab a teaspoon, rather than waiting until midnight to eat their Müller Fruit Corner.

TommyK: squirting ketchup eyes and a smile onto the dinner plate of a loved one before serving, because even though you're both grown-ups you can still be adorable.

Trolleystabble: a brief flash of murderous rage on aisle three of a supermarket when a loved one tries to hurry you out of the store with an 'Are we finished yet?', mistaking the weekly big shop for your own personal, slightly self-indulgent leisure pursuit.

Walkergasm: a sinister atmosphere that enters the room when someone announces 'plain' as their favourite crisp flavour.

Welcome Breakdown: a life-sabotaging compulsion 280 metres after joining any British motorway that you must ruin your schedule with a stop for a Zinger Tower meal and a mooch around a Waitrose Mini.

Will-I-Aming: putting crisps in a ramekin because it's Saturday at 6 p.m., but no other time.

Willywumbling: The creeping realisation most of us have as adults that Willy Wonka was possibly some sort of sinister pervert, but we'd have gone to the factory anyway for the everlasting gobstoppers.

Wubblegunt: the soft squidgy primordial purse that hangs over your underwear elastic which you could lose in about three weeks by stopping your Pud in a Mug habit, but quite frankly you haven't got room in your life for this negativity.

Acknowledgements

Writing books turns me into an enormous bore. I choose difficult topics that make me revisit painful things, and then attempt to write about them in a jolly way involving Findus Crispy Pancakes. I make copious notes, pin spider graphs to fridges and leave uncapped Sharpies everywhere, including the bed. I spend days lying horizontal, mewling pitifully about 'my art' and 'waiting for the muse to strike' while forgetting everyone's birthday. I wake at 5 a.m., slurp pints of Gold Blend coffee, clank loudly on my laptop, then expect a medal for doing my job, for which I've quite literally been paid in 'advance', spent already on sparkly shoes.

I would like to beg clemency from the following people:

Cathryn Summerhayes – my poor literary agent.

The fabulous Mo Hafeez and the entire, very patient, team at Faber Books.

The long suffering Charles – partner, chauffeur, therapist.

Courtney Arumugam, Matt Park and Tom Gormer – my squad, who make every day doable.

The legendary Hugh Smithson-Wright: always awake at dawn for a rambling voicenote.

Milly Bell, Alex Segal at Intertalent.

Bob Granleese and Tim Lusher at the *Guardian*.

And not least of all:

David, Tam, Lola Dent and Bob Watts for allowing me to talk about stuff that happened.

You are all amazing and very loved. Thank you.